Indian Diaspora Handbook

Mental Health Challenges & Solutions

2nd Edition

Greesh C. Sharma, Ph.D., DMSP

Second Edition – Aug 2015

First Printing 2013

ISBN: 978-0-9886516-0-9

Mental illness does not limit its havoc to the brain and mind, but it goes far beyond, affecting health, well-being, longevity, integrity of the family, marriage, and parenting, not to mention national productivity and pride.

Contents

Foreword

Health is wealth, and mental health is not only personal wealth, but also the wealth of the society, the country, and the world. It is a well-known fact that a sound mind in a sound body makes a wholesome person. A society composed of physically strong and emotionally integrated people will prosper.

This well-researched practical handbook by Dr. Greesh Sharma, a longstanding practicing clinical psychologist, is about mental-health challenges with special reference to the Indian Diaspora living in the US and around the world. The contribution of the Indian Diaspora–with their thousands of years of cultural and spiritual background in the countries to which they have migrated–is immense, but they, because of the society around them, are also subject to severe mental challenges.

Indians living in India are also affected by the mindless modernity or the alien cultures in India brought there by invaders and, more recently, by the British rule. The British rule intimidated Indians to the extent that they felt inferior and readily accepted many things that were imported, considering that the latter was better than what was indigenous. This is deeply ingrained in Indians even now.

A substantial part of the book deals with the demography of India and the countries to which Indians have emigrated. Dr. Sharma expresses his fear that, if Indians, with their generally passive attitude, ignore the changes brought by adversaries, the thousands of years of Indian civilization and their identity may be lost.

"Silently suffering is the second nature of Indians. Hindus view suffering as a result of external factors over which one has no control, so why bother?"

Hindus also apply *Karma Siddhanta* whenever they feel helpless, instead of confronting the problem head on. This has been perhaps the leading reason India is near the top of the list of countries with suicide cases.

For the Indian Diaspora, life revolves around work, income, professional success, academic performance, fame, and name in the society. Parents are highly focused on achievement and expect their children to succeed in school and college, and, ultimately, in their professions. This rat-race to succeed professionally, materially and monetarily is gaining intensity among the Diaspora, thus leading to pressure, stress, and ailments related to the mind. To de-stress themselves, members of the Diaspora more frequently become addicted to alcohol and drugs. In fact, drinking alcohol has become a status symbol in Diaspora society.

Looking from a Hindu perspective, Dr. Sharma says that Hindus do not view addiction as a disease but as a habituated desire for pleasure. But this pleasure-seeking leads to addiction and, in addiction, pleasure and pain are tied together. Finally, pain dominates the pleasure. As a professional psychologist, the author suggests 12 steps, applying Sankhya-Yoga of Hindu philosophy to treat addiction.

Here, the author sounds a warning to the Diaspora. Indians living abroad are increasingly engaging in addictions, criminal behaviors, displaying violence & acting out sexually. The author interestingly presents a broad list of mental illnesses and personality characteristics of Indian psychopaths, citing their case histories.

Writing about Indians and their mental health, and quoting an Indian patient, Dr. Sharma says: "Indian people do not take mental-health professionals seriously, and fear stigma and social ostracism." We need to educate Indian patients, he suggests, on the nature of the mental-health profession, the benefits of counseling, and the consequence of not seeking help.

As Indian immigrant populations have been rapidly growing in various countries, they continue to feel torn between Indian and Western values. These differences engender emotional distress among immigrants and lead to an increasing crime rate.

Indian parents, wary of their children taking to Western lifestyles, including dating, put many restrictions on their sons and daughters. Often, however, their children resent their parents' interference. This leads to aggressive and erratic behavior.

Indian parents have difficulty dealing with their children's mental disorders or depression. They rigidly deal with their offspring in traditional parenting ways rather than reach out for professional help and accept the treatments that work.

In such situations, writes Dr. Sharma, it is not good enough for Indians to be proud of their Vedas, Indian medicine, or vegetarianism. What they need is for their depressed children to receive appropriate treatment.

As mental disorders vary in nature, so, too, do their treatments. As each patient is unique, so, too, must his or her treatment be planned and administered according to individual needs.

Dr. Sharma urges a three-phased approach in treating Indian patients. The first phase includes initial diagnostic interviews and observations. The middle phase consists of educating patients about their diagnoses, as patients typically need help neutralizing their negative feelings which may impede treatment. In the final phase, as the risk of abrupt termination, non-compliance, or no-show for treatment is high, therapists must educate patients about the process of therapy termination.

Patients should be encouraged to make a list of post-treatment goals. The list should be specific, simple, and relevant to the treatment. If the patient makes this investment, follow-up sessions should be scheduled.

Psychotropic and antiepileptic medications are rather expensive. Therapists must educate patients about these facts as well as possible side effects including drug dependence.

Of course, medications are not substitutes for psychotherapy, nor is psychotherapy a substitute for medications. Therapists must clearly point out that some medications (Anxiolytic) are addictive and others are effective only for limited periods and hence need to be repeated to sustain results. Therapists should tell patients that medication and psychotherapy treatments are not a pure science and must be approached in a trial-and-error fashion. A team approach to treatment is more effective and provides the necessary checks and balances that ensure caring for the patient as a whole person.

Self-help therapeutic solutions for mental-health issues for Indians may be necessary as many Indians view psychotherapy as a taboo. The goal of such therapy should not be to strengthen therapeutic dependence, but rather to create non-dependence or autonomy, allowing the patient to develop the "therapist within."

Self-help solutions are numerous in the U.S. There is a National Mental-Health Self-Help Clearing House that links individuals to self-help solutions. There are also foundations specializing in disorders such as depression, bipolar, and schizophrenia, and these agencies can provide relevant information. The National Alliance for the Mentally Ill (NAMI) provides self-help resources to patients and their families.

The book discusses the limitations of conventional therapy and self-help solutions for mental illnesses. It notes that the main impediment to professional treatment is its cost. Therefore, mental-health services are not accessible to most people.

Professionally-trained treatment providers include psychiatrists, psychologists, counselors, and social workers. All these mental-health providers have their individual roles to play. Psychiatrists see mental problems as disorders of brain chemistry or the product of some physical etiology. Psychologists, if need be, do not hesitate to refer patients for psychiatric and neurological consultations so the patients may receive comprehensive and effective treatment. In treating the patients, licensed professional counselors and social workers also play an effective role.

Unlike the Western model of eight stages of development, Indians categorize development as four ashrams – Brahmacharya, Grihastha, Vanaprastha, and Sanyasa. In each ashrama, one goes through a specific developmental process. At the final Sanyasa stage, one prepares oneself for the final journey with the practice of Sankhya-Yoga's eight stages of Yama, Niyama, Asana, Pranayama, Pratyahara, Dharna, Dhyan, and Samadhi.

The author explains the process of an individual's changes and developments within his mind, body, and behavior. For an individual to achieve tranquility of mind and body, Dr. Sharma lists self-help techniques, such as self-discipline; *samkalpa* or resolve; fasting to give mind and body a break; relaxation to arouse the para-sympathetic nervous system; cognitive restructuring through meditation, mantra, and breathing exercises; living in the moment or the ability to balance the thoughts of past, present, and future; and engaging in rituals like performing pooja, meeting distinguished persons, or going on a pilgrimage.

Dr. Sharma lists several types of mental and psychological disorders, including specific disorders suffered by the Indian Diaspora because of their cross-cultural exposure; and he advocates Indian ways to Western ways in treating the psychological disorders of members of the Diaspora. His argument is based on the fact that Western psychology, with its limitations, has a relatively short history of about 100 years, while Indian psychological knowledge is comprehensive, which is thousands of years old based on *Vedas*.

Sharma writes: "The Vedic psychotherapy embodies the oldest known clinical procedures used to help human beings deal with their feelings as well as the dilemmas of life, death, growth, and Nirvana (liberation)." He adds that Western psychotherapy is Rational-Emotive Therapy (RET), Cognitive Behavioral Therapy (CBT), or Behavior Modification, each of which has a single-minded focus. In contrast, Vedic psychotherapy holistically addresses cognitive restructuring, habit and behavior changes, and the integration of spirituality.

This book is the result of Dr. Sharma's fund of knowledge about psychology and his years of exhaustive experience as a clinical psychologist. It carries comprehensive information about mental disorders, with specific reference to the Indian Diaspora.

J.V. Lakshmana Rao

J.V. Lakshmana Rao, for the past 18 years, has been the Editor of the Chicago-based India Tribune, one of the oldest nationwide Indian newspapers. Prior to that, he worked in India, with Indian Express, Deccan Chronicle, West Coast Times and The Hitawada, spanning over 30 years. He may be contacted at rao@indiatribune.com.

Preface

My fascination with Indians has been intense since my early childhood. Initially, it was simply my visceral reaction to having read Indian history as a student and concluding that Indians were perpetually victimized. It was constantly driven home to me how Greeks, Turks, Kushans, Huns, Persians, and Muslim marauders from central Asia could come on a whim and raid the heartland of the country with no serious resistance, violent reactions, dire repercussions or harm. This process of India's cultural rape and the details of a Hindu holocaust triggered in me a very strong desire to understand what it is about Indians that draws them to tolerate victimization and subjugation, and the acceptance of neverending apathy. Indian apathy and resistance to change extend beyond any rational analysis. At the same time, I am fascinated as to what made the Mongols, British, Portuguese, and French so successful in colonizing and exploiting India, and in the process destroying a uniquely ancient *mother of all civilizations.*

The simple explanation is that the Hindu belief system makes Indians choose non-reactivity which leads to apathy, leaving non-Hindu and foreign adversaries empowered and superior due to their pragmatic tactics, unscrupulous violence, and self-serving manipulations. This creates a double-edged sword. If Hindus become like their enemies, then their civilization will cease to be unique and enduring. Ironically, if Hindus do not respond to their adversaries in kind, Indian civilization will cease to exist due to a loss of identity, fragmentation, and partitioning of India again and again.

This dilemma has rarely been contemplated, examined critically, or debated by Indians. Indian indifference and apathy are continuing in spite of full cognizance that the globalization phenomenon is digging the final grave of whatever is left of Indian civilization. The issue of the decline of Hindu civilization is serious enough to require some examination. This conclusion has prompted me to explore the dynamics of the Indian national character, mental health dilemmas, and preferred coping mechanisms, as well as the strength and resilience Indians display. What started out as merely an interest in Indian history later became a passion to feel, touch, hear, and experience India. My choice of becoming a psychologist, and the opportunity to see Indian patients in private practice lead me to explore and better understand the Indian personality and interpersonal dynamics. The Indian patient population is varied and is represented by men and women, children and elderly, individuals, couples and family units from almost every province of India. Additionally, I also saw patients from Trinidad, Fiji, Mauritius, Bangladesh, Pakistan and many other countries of the Diaspora.

My leading and coordinating the Vanaprastha Corps', an interdisciplinary psychological-medical-addiction treatment program for the Indian Diaspora, has allowed me to interact with wide and diverse communities both clinically and socially. Usually, these Projects were in the form of Mental Health-Medical-Addiction treatment camps that also included teaching, training, and consulting in various countries of the Indian Diaspora.

It has always been my passion to experience the essence of India, whether traveling within India from Kashmir to Kanyakumari, from Andaman to Ajmer or visiting all the nations where the Indian Diaspora has settled. These journeys have taken me to crisscrossing the Silk Route, Alexander the Great's campaign route, retracing Mahatma Gandhi's footsteps, visiting Tinganes (the smallest capital in the world), making a pilgrimage through villages where ancient Aramaic is spoken, traveling to the Muslim shrines from Syria to Pakistan, exploring Jesus' life from Jerusalem, Bethlehem to Egypt, and climbing the mountaintops of Kailash at almost 20,000 feet in Tibet. I have crisscrossed the equator at least three times as well as traveled to the ends of the earth from Cape of Horn to Cape of Good Hope.

This book is dedicated to the Indian Diaspora and the mental health consumers and providers now or in the making. Mental health for the Indian Diaspora is a recent development, and it will be a slow process before the community learns to utilize it adequately. Stigma and lack of familiarity as to psychologists'/ psychiatrists' roles are major obstacles. Similarly, Indian mental health providers are so few and far in-between that they are unable to serve wherever there is a need for them. Indian mental health practitioners have yet to take it upon themselves to educate the community at large. They are in the first phase of establishing themselves as mental health entrepreneurs.

Mainstream media continues to report all Diasporic illegal acts as crimes instead of pointing out that many of them are simply acts of manic-depression, addictions, schizophrenia, and psychopathic personalities. As a result, dually diagnosable Indians end up in the prison system without any advocacy or support. In essence, the Indian Diaspora at large has yet to recognize the importance of good mental health as a prerequisite for marital, familial, intergenerational, and individual empowerment and well-being. Spirituality begins where good mental health ends, and happiness is experienced only when one is free from physical and mental distress.

Greesh C. Sharma,
Yardley, Pennsylvania,
August 15th, 2015

Acknowledgments

Clinical psychology would not have become my passion without the inspiration of my deceased cousin, Yogendra Shanker Sharma. I would never have aspired to become a devout student of clinical psychology if not for the nurturing of Professor J.G. Tripathi. And I would have never acquired the trait to accept challenges without the provocations of Professor Jai J. Tiwari, both in the Psychology Department at Varshney College, Aligarh, UP. I was not alone in my inspirations, but I was the only one who excelled beyond their dreams.

My lifelong ambition was to become a respected psychologist but I was unsure how that would come about. It was partly my perseverance, but also, in reality a coincidence that I entered a clinical psychology internship. Of course, it was my dream to become a clinical psychologist in the true sense and not just an academician and an armchair theorist. I learned about such a clinical program that would make me a legitimate psychologist through a friend of a relative, and decided to mail a postcard to the Ministry of Health, Government of India, requesting a scholarship at the National Institute of Mental Health and Neurosciences (NIMHNS) in Bengaluru, in South India. I was late by two months in applying. All I did was write a postcard expressing my desire. But I received the most amazing reply, an offer to join the Institute immediately. My scholarship was a meager INR.200 i.e. $4.50 per month. But for me it was the ticket to my ultimate destination and an affirmation of a life-changing miracle. I graduated in February 1968. In emotional terms, this gave me a niche and a sense of legitimacy. For the first time, I felt I had a clear destination.

The rest is a history of hard work, unfailing self-discipline, uphill struggles, the strangest possible challenges, overwhelming traumas, and endless uncertainties. It all had a purpose, in shaping up my adulthood, and in manifesting the destiny which, fortunately, brought me to the United States. Before I came to the USA, my father suffered a sudden and painful death. It became my responsibility to provide for, educate my three siblings, and to see them properly married, and, of course, I needed to look after my mother.

The time following my arrival in the USA was even more challenging since I only came with $7.00, like most immigrants of the 1970s, and no friends, family, or support system. In pursuit of my psychology career in the USA, I encountered major struggles, hurts, humiliations, traumas, challenges, and threats, as well as successes, learned lessons, and inspirations. There were people in authority who displayed outright prejudice, and I had felt discriminated against, but there were others who nurtured me and became my unforgettable mentors. Working at the Trenton Psychiatric Hospital, New Jersey starting on June 8, 1970, was the humble beginning. In time, I rose to procure hospital privileges in dozens of hospitals, joining the staff of many nursing homes and eventually engaging in a full-time and very rewarding private practice. Psychiatric hospitals during those days were primitive, similar to the depiction in the movie *Snake Pit*.

On the other hand, they were also the sanctuaries for foreign mental health graduates. General hospitals were mainly under the control of white Americans, and of course they were dynasties for and by medical doctors. Getting into private practice was positively another life-altering decision. It was an amazing journey and times were historically significant. Clinical psychology in the USA during the 1970s until 2000 was struggling to separate itself from religion and a "wishy-washy", unrecognized, "artsy-craftsy", disrespected, informal, poor man's science. It was not even known as a profession then. The entire profession was insecure and had no clear sense of its role, place, and acceptance by others. A collective insecurity, inferiority, and self-doubts were the modus operandi for psychologists at the time. We all talked too much and wrote elaborate reports, not because they were necessary, but merely to compensate for our inner inadequacies.

Verbosity was the veneer to hide everything we felt negative about ourselves as psychologists. When psychologists participated—during ward rounds, case conferences, or radio interviews—or when asked for an opinion, we talked incessantly and intellectually, conveying insecurity and over-compensation for our professional sense of incompetence. It was amazing to be part of three decades of psychology's rise as a mainstream profession, and above all becoming established enough to serve the masses independent of a medical and psychiatric monopoly.

Now that five decades have passed, American psychologists—unlike those in India, Europe, and Third World countries—have become a model for psychology professionals elsewhere. The need to compensate by hyperbole is today replaced with the precision of a medical model. The struggle to become unique by obsessing with psychometry has dissipated. Psychologists have given up internal fighting or jealous competition and can work as a team. They emerged from mental hospitals to general hospitals, military settings, nursing homes, and prisons, and their services became relevant from birth-to-death. The concept of psychology practice became promising and financially rewarding. The growth and popularity were so rapid that psychologists contemplated privileges to prescribe psychotropics, indirectly threatening psychiatrists' monopoly. I am proud to be a part of the history of having represented psychology on a personal level and using my Indian academic credentials in dozens of institutions.

Eventually, I was appointed as Assistant Hospital Administrator and as a Licensed Nursing Home Administrator. Additionally, I was granted privileges as a Hindu clergy at the Capital Health Systems, the first-ever clergy of Hindu background to serve Hindu patients in the hospital system.

I would be remiss if I didn't warmly acknowledge the contribution of my biological family, psychologically significant others, tons of colleagues and friends, and over thirty thousand patients. The contribution of patients in therapists' success is priceless as we get paid twice; first monetarily and second through emotional growth. The role of my wife, Olga (Urmila) Sharma has been extremely crucial. I would not have realized my potential without her support, loving confrontations, daily teasing, and inspiration. As deadlines to finish the book loomed, I sought escape in traveling and playing chef, but she managed to bring me back to reality. This completed book is one example of her relentless rigorousness. I am glad she was on my side.

Being a clinical psychologist was much easier than writing the book. The writing was an organic process full of trial and error lasting over five years. I lacked experience, and also time, due to my busy practice and other endless obligations. However, the decision to finally have skilled friends help with the project made it all emerge in black and white. I cannot describe in words the assistance Kate Casper provided. She proved to be an angel as she patiently edited the second edition which was overdue. My daughter Bharati Sharma assisted me with proof-reading of the book despite being busy with her wedding preparations. Amanda Reed's careful review and spellchecking saved ample time. Keshav Basavapatna's skillful assistance was very valuable. Kumar Tadepalli's assistance with each and every aspect of the book from editing, formatting and ePublishing finally brought this book into reality. Divya Basavapatna created the book cover. I hope the book proves worthwhile and serves the targeted Diaspora; so much effort, goodwill and sacrifice of so many people have enriched it.

Introduction

This book is a primer about the collective mental health of the more than one billion members of what has come to be called the Indian Diaspora. This huge mass of unique humanity shares a particular gestalt, regardless of caste, region, province, language, religion, & infinite sub-cultural diversity. Among three major civilizations, China, Egypt, and India, it is the latter that has retained the most continuous collective characteristics of a civilization. China buckled under the communist Cultural Revolution, and Egypt lost its originality under the influence of Islam. Persian civilization had its epic, but now it's insignificant due to its very small population.

> *"Present-day India is not a new civilization on an ancient soil, like Iran or Egypt. The living stream of Indian consciousness in the twentieth century is continuity, the same stream which has been steadily flowing for millennia. The Pyramids speak of the glory of an Egypt that is gone; the Mohenjo Daro is not a relic but an organism in the living culture of India."*

Srimati Sophia Wadia: The Path of Satyagraha

India remains a complex gestalt that combines a deeply ingrained commonality of personality traits, uniformity of core character, predictable behavioral patterns, and indispensable core values. I have often heard that *you can take Indians out of India but not the India out of Indians*. Even when transplanted abroad, their being rooted in "Indainness" guides their mind-body and life.

India has had severe blows to its psyche, social order, and national character because of a past that includes thousands of years of foreign rule. Indian history is rife with traumas of holocaust proportion. The genocide and the premeditated destruction of the Hindu libraries, universities, places of religious worship, cities, and towns was carried out, namely from the Tatars, Persians, Uzbeks, Mongols, Afghans, Portuguese, and British. The

Hindu genocide continues to date unabated in Kashmir, Bangladesh, and Pakistan. Jews and Armenians got the recognition of their holocaust, but Hindus still wait to be recognized and considered a threatened species.

The Indian word for crisis is *aapati*, meaning holocaust, total catastrophe, doom, gloom, danger, and utter helplessness, beyond the ability to defend. It is worth noting that only people suffering from post-traumatic stress disorder (PTSD) tend to define threats, danger, and crisis in such terms. The Chinese word for crisis implies dangerousness plus opportunity. Modern marauders come to India in the guise of proselytizers and terrorists perpetuating the after effects of PTSD and chipping away the Hindus' identity. Among the entire global Indian Diaspora, Hindu identity shows the most pervasive traumatization and atrophy.

Those in power usually, but not always non-Indians, have dictated the norms of everyday living and thinking. With this mass hypnosis in effect, Indians have lived apathetically and without purpose, managing to control only one moment at a time. This has been the Indian condition for over 1,000 years. Lately, the statistics that were used by outsiders in the past are being employed by current governments, in spite of their being Indians themselves.

"Where the clear stream of reason
has not lost its way into the
dreary desert sand of dead habit;
where the mind is lead forward
by the intro ever-widening
thought and action-
into that heaven of freedom
my Father
let my country awake."

- Rabindranath Tagore

However, it's not all gloom and doom. Despite the external influences, Indians have spread all over the world and have resiliently managed the external context via their ingenuity, peaceful coexistence and cultural spirituality. Although their political and economic status varies greatly from country to country, the overall image of the Diaspora is one that is positive and often emulated. For one hundred plus years, members have made significant contributions to their respective lands of adoption. Without exception, they tend to be a model minority, never victimizing other minorities, resorting to violence, nor putting down people of other faiths. They live unpretentiously as to their wealth, education, or accomplishments. It is a group that, in general, does not create waves and prefers to accomplish very quietly and discreetly, deflecting all attention and remaining focused on the basics of life.

Beneath the surface, despite this group's immense accomplishments, is an underlying collective emotional syndrome that is largely rooted in the mother country's long history of political subjugation, being rendered helpless and relentless assault on core identity. This history has left deep emotional scars on the psyche of the Indian Diaspora. These scars reveal themselves in symptoms such as self-denigration, self-doubt, apathy, passivity, denial, minimization of challenges and distancing from threats, and the veneer of compensatory delusional sense of self-importance to cover up collective sense of vulnerability.

"The key of India is in London."
Benjamin Disraeli: Speech, House of Lords,
March 5, 1881

On an individual level, this sense of insecurity manifests itself in the form of apathy, passivity; minimal involvement and avoidance of seeing the "bigger psycho-socio-political picture". Such naiveté leaves the Diaspora members a soft target for abuse by aggressive locals, racist minorities, or power hungry social groups. In Kenya, natives saw Indians as traitors because they never invested in land but instead held their funds in the UK which was contrary to the Kenyans' cultural values. In Africa and elsewhere, Indians related to the Blacks only as labor, and not at a household level. Additionally, apathy even to their own feelings manifests in difficulties managing their own emotional needs and challenges. As a group, Indians exhibit extreme loyalty to the extended family, but paradoxically, they have great difficulty acting collectively for the greater good of the Diaspora community. On a national level, this insecurity reveals itself in how India relates to the rest of the world, which is often through the prism of seeking acceptance and avoiding confrontation. Nothing in India or about Indians is good enough unless the former colonial bosses (Europeans) or their cousin Americans say "it is good." Plenty of national energy and resources are wasted in this futile attempt to seek a stamp of foreigners' approval. Yoga became acceptable to Indians only after it became a buzzword in the West.

The thesis of this book is that it is no longer sufficient to rest on the laurels of "India shining", or claims of India's past glory, nor the claim that it is the most ancient living culture, having invented numerals, Buddhism, and so much more. The country's technical competence and military buildup is indeed impressive but has done little to ease the suffering of either the Indian masses or that

> "Johan Galtung, a leading practitioner, agrees with Lindner that the infliction of humiliation is a profoundly violent psychological act that leaves the victim with a deep wound to the psyche."
>
> Lindner, Evelin G.
> *Humiliation or Dignity*

of its displaced, depressed, and traumatized countrymen abroad. Nothing makes sense unless good mental health becomes a priority for the Diaspora.

There is a morbid disconnect among Indians ranging from the operators of the Indian Government to the smallest level of managing a temple or a community center. Even when governments of the Indian Diaspora abroad, run by elected officials who are Indians, the government of India avoids any responsible involvement, moral or cultural. Whenever there is a natural catastrophe or political-ethnic victimization of Indians, the government of India acts brain-dead. The arrest of the elected Prime Minister Mahendra Chaudhry of Fiji (2009) because he was

Indian, the murder of hundreds of Indians in Malaysia during riots and ethnic violence, and the ethnic cleansing of Hindus in Pakistan, Bangladesh and Uganda never even brought a condemnation from the Prime Minister of India or by the Indian Muslims. This apathy and paradoxical detachment are a byproduct of the colonial mindset, rooted in the fear of making a mistake, being seen as biased, or facing foreign criticism.

Yes, Caste systems cause mental problems. The Caste system is the worst form of hierarchy, causing or contributing to chronic stress, depression, damaged self-esteem and post-traumatic stress disorders among the most vulnerable individuals in Indian Society. Invented by Hindus, it's pervasive even among Indian Muslims and Christians. Clinical psychologists have a very important role to play in prevention and treatment as well as in educating the larger society to be sensitive.

While bureaucrats and politicians do their thing, scientists sit in their labs, and professors take comfort in their ivory towers; the Diaspora feels increasingly defenseless and exhausted. A new generation of social scientists must evolve to address the emotional, spiritual, and social needs of the Indian Diaspora. These triumphs remain hollow unless new affronts to individual well-being, marital harmony, and family unity are addressed. The somewhat unique phenomenon of Hindu individualism plays a crucial role in their self-perception, how they define and relate to others, how they perceive the world, and in practical terms, how they relate to the larger politics, inter-racial and inter-ethnic issues. These subjective perceptions and idealism-based handling of reality has pervasive and long-term implications for the Diaspora.

This book is a modest attempt to do just that. It is based on my academic and clinical education in India, my work and practice as a psychotherapist in the USA since 1970, my having lived in cross-cultural settings, and my visits to more than 121 countries. The best way to get the most out of this book is to consider it as a stepping stone, a basic guide to be complemented by reading other books, and even better, undergoing therapeutic experience. I hope this will facilitate one's personal growth as well as empowering, supporting and nurturing the India Diaspora.

One caveat for the reader, when I use the word "Indian," I am referring specifically to more than 80% of the population of the Diaspora who are Hindus. I am very well aware of the inter-religious sensitivities and the differences. I am well versed in realizing that Muslim identity's ideal is to be like Prophet Mohammad (of Arabia) (PBUH), and that Christian molding is Euro-centric (Roman Catholic, Syrian, Greek Orthodox, Russian, or Mormon). However, scrutiny indicates that Hindus have exerted significant influence on other communities to create a certain amount of national uniformity called "Indianness." What is said of the Hindus here may also, to a large extent, apply to or be true of other Indian minorities in India or the larger Diaspora. The twenty-first century and globalization has resulted in a rather significant psychological and social assimilation. Let us take a simple example. The upper caste, Hindus who converted to Christianity in Kerala, are known to demand that converted Hindus from lower and Dalit castes must have their own and separate Churches. In essence, regardless of the religion, it seems that the caste system in some or other fashion seems to be synonymous with Indians. In Islam too there is supposed to be no caste system, but a close scrutiny shows that the Indian Muslim community is replete with class and caste-like hierarchies, pecking orders and prejudices.

Background: The Indian Diaspora

The sun never sets on the Indian Diaspora. The Indian disbursement did not begin with the British. It is as old as time itself. What is different now is that every seventh person on earth is an Indian. Rulers, colonials, and armies have come and gone, but India manages to sustain its democracy, spirituality, and ancient civilization. India is always evolving and patiently waiting for the world to grow beyond its infantilism and adolescence, before returning to the roots of Vasudhaiva Kutumbkam. The world is one big family.

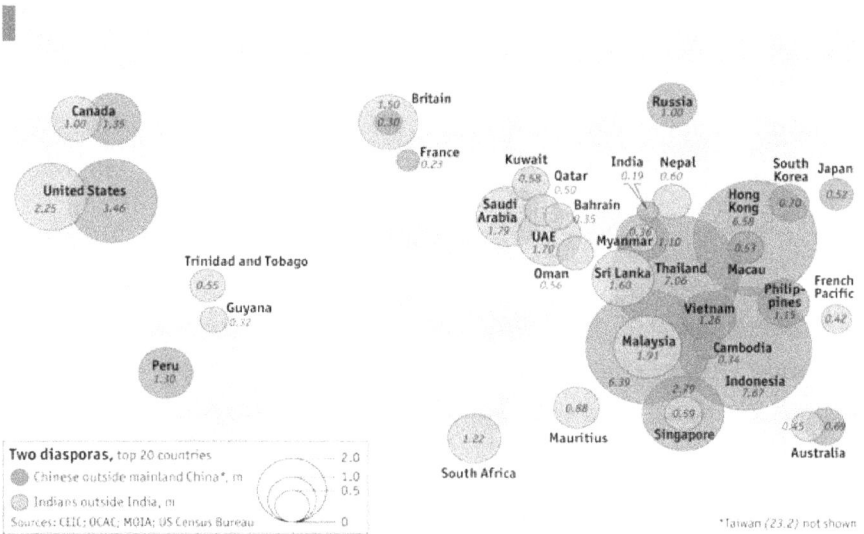

Canada 1.00 1.35
United States 2.25 1.46
Trinidad and Tobago 0.55
Guyana 0.32
Peru 1.30
Britain 1.50 0.10
France 0.23
South Africa 1.22
Kuwait 0.58 Qatar 0.50
Saudi Arabia 1.29
Bahrain 0.35
UAE 1.70
Oman 0.56
India 0.19 Nepal 0.60
Myanmar 1.10
Sri Lanka 1.68 Thailand 2.06
Vietnam 1.26
Malaysia 1.91 6.39
Cambodia 0.34
Mauritius 0.88
Singapore 0.69 2.79
Indonesia 7.87
South Korea Japan 0.52
Hong Kong 6.58 0.63
Macau
Philip-pines 1.15 French Pacific 0.42
Russia 3.00
Australia 0.45 0.69

Two diasporas, top 20 countries
Chinese outside mainland China*, m
Indians outside India, m
Sources: CEIC; OCAC; MOIA; US Census Bureau
2.0 1.0 0.5 0

*Taiwan (23.2) not shown

There are an estimated 30,000,000 people of Indian origin living outside of India. According to the United Nations Development Program, this gives India the second largest Diaspora in the world, after China. This number includes non-resident Indians, or Indian citizens who have migrated elsewhere, were born outside of India, or who live permanently outside India. It also includes Persons of Indian Origin (PIO) who live outside of the country but are not citizens of India.

These overseas Indians reside in significant quantities in 48 countries. In eight of these countries–Malaysia, Myanmar, Saudi Arabia, South Africa, Sri Lanka, UAE, the United Kingdom, and the United States—they number more than a million. In other countries, they represent sizeable percentages of the overall population. They represent the largest ethnic community in Mauritius (79%), Guyana (59%), Fiji (49%), Trinidad and Tobago (40%), and Suriname (37%). They form substantial minorities in countries like Hong Kong, Malaysia, Singapore, Sri Lanka, and South and East Africa, and have a significant presence in Australia, Canada, the United Kingdom, and the United States.

Although most scholars refer to two or three major waves of Indian migration, it is important to remember that Indians have been traveling to other countries for thousands of years. For example, during the first century A.D., the so-called "trade diaspora" took place, in which trade networks between India and the Southeast Asian countries of Burma, Laos, Thailand, Cambodia, Malaysia, Indonesia, and Sri Lanka resulted in Indian settlements. The influence of Indian culture is still strongly felt in this part of the world, and can be clearly seen in the lasting influence of Vedic and Hindu culture throughout the region and in Hindu temple architecture. Witness the Cambodian Angkor Wat and the Batu Caves in Malaysia, the former being the largest Hindu temple complex in the world, and the latter being one of the most popular Hindu shrines outside India.

Beyond these ancient migrations, what is most commonly referred to as the Indian Diaspora took place during and after the colonial era when India was ruled by the British.

During the colonial period from approximately 1830 to 1873, the British outlawed slavery and sought out cheap replacements for the freed slaves who worked labor-intensive industries in plantation economies in East Africa and countries that included Mauritius, Guyana, the Caribbean, Fiji, and East Africa. During this phase, Indians primarily from Uttar Pradesh and Bihar worked under contract in slave-like conditions in such places as the sugar plantations of the Caribbean, the rubber plantations of Malaysia, and the railroad projects of East Africa.

This system of indentured labor followed, and in some cases paralleled, the Kangani system of labor, during which Indian middlemen mediated between Indian laborers and plantation owners in South Asia. Workers were overwhelmingly Tamilians from South India and had kinship alliances to the Kangani middlemen's village, kin, or caste group.

The migrations in the post-colonial period were entirely different from the earlier forms of migration, in that the conditions of migrations were more voluntary and qualitatively less predatory. This includes the skilled and unskilled workers who moved to the Gulf States and other parts of West Asia during the oil-boom of 1973-1974, and the middle-class, highly skilled, technically elite who moved en masse to the developed nations of the West, especially in the late 1960s and early 1970s.

As can be seen from this brief survey, emigrants from India are a heterogeneous lot. Migrant circumstances create a variety of factors that include numbers of migrants, periods of migration, treatment by their host countries, their regional and linguistic backgrounds, and the orientation of the Diasporic Indians to their native land. As William Safran notes (2005), it is a general characteristic of diasporics that "they continue to relate, personally or vicariously, to their homeland in one way or another, and their ethno-communal consciousness and solidarity are importantly defined by the existence of such a relationship."(37)

Despite the common perception that overseas Indians are a prosperous breed, it is important to understand that many of the 30 million Hindus living outside of India are subject to discrimination, terror, violence, forced conversions, ethnic cleansing, socio-political ostracization, and disenfranchisement. In some countries, fundamentalists advance a discriminatory and non-inclusive agenda and promote hatred of religious and ethnic minorities. As far as mental health services are concerned, these countries do not see it as a priority as they are in the initial stages of econo-political development. Their priorities and resources are directed by political motivations and not the somato-psycho-socio-spiritual needs of the masses. In this regard, developed countries like the USA, Canada, and the UK have more experience and offer shortcuts to developing mental health service blueprints. I have visited most countries that are home to the Indian Diaspora and in some of these there is not even a single available mental health professional. The mentally ill are still treated either as if they are possessed by evil spirits, as criminals, or simply ignored. In some countries, however, the medical profession is slowly evolving to acquaint itself with mental illnesses and has begun to act as gatekeepers.

"Mental Health represents one of the last frontiers in the improvement of the human condition. In the face of wide-spread stigma and inattention, mental health must now be placed on the international agenda."
Jimmy and Rosalynn Carter, from their forward titled *The World Mental Health Report.*

The advocacy group Hindu America Foundation (HAF) conducts surveys on the state of human rights in Asian diasporic countries, many of which in recent years have exhibited racist policies towards Indians. Capsule summaries from their 2011 report can be found in Appendix A, and their recommendations in Appendix B. This information is included here because human rights violations cause irreparable psychological damage to the minorities and victims ranging from mental breakdown to relinquishing their religious faith, traditions, and culture. They feel coerced to give up their identity to protect their women, children, and elders.

PEOPLE'S REPUBLIC OF BANGLADESH

I visited Bangladesh during the third week of February 2000. During my encounters with numerous Hindu families, I learned that they felt vulnerable, unsafe, depressed, traumatized, and desperate. Their collective sense of post-traumatic stress disorder is rooted in reality, as the absence of law and order and victimization by fundamentalists and criminals have made many feel unable to continue living in that country. They feel they cannot protect their women and children or practice Hinduism due to Muslim interference. At the same time, they feel abandoned by India and the Hindu Diaspora at large. Mental health services are minimal, and social stigmatization keeps them from seeking help.

KINGDOM OF BHUTAN

I visited Bhutan during the second week of February 2005. On the surface, the country was peaceful and welcoming. I was surprised to learn later that Hindus have been exiled and discriminated against in large numbers. I have met many Hindu Bhutanese refugees in the USA. On the whole, they seem a happy people but are traumatized by their poverty and being forced to come and live in an unfamiliar culture. In Bhutan, there were no mental health services available, except those that were informally carried out by Buddhist monks.

REPUBLIC OF THE FIJI ISLANDS

I visited Fiji in October of 1996. During my lecture tour there, I was fortunate enough to have personal and trusting interactions with native blacks but also many Indians. The dynamics were fascinating. There was no mutual trust or respect. Native blacks saw Indians as greedy, money-minded, and arrogant while Indians saw blacks as unreliable, untrustworthy, and unaccountable. I learned that most Indians own businesses and when they have black employees, they expect them to open the business on time, be there, and handle their personal life before or after work. However, due to the natives' tribal roots, they have little awareness of time or punctuality. They live based on their moods and feelings. For example, if there is a death in the tribal village, they may not show up to work for months. I have observed this dilemma in most countries where Indians have settled and blacks are natives or in significant number.

INDIAN STATE OF JAMMU AND KASHMIR

I visited Srinagar in 2004. I have never seen any place on Earth so heavily militarized. Most Hindus have been pushed out, and even the local Muslim population is afraid of Islamists. During one of my conversations, a local Muslim teacher—in a soft whisper due to fear—shared with me that in his view, Muslims have been extremely unfair to Kashmiri Pundits. If Islamization of Kashmir is a sample as to what happens to minorities, it may be a sign of future mental health calamity for other religious groups. I have spoken to a few Kashmir refugees in the USA who are clearly demonstrating symptoms of depression and post trauma.

MALAYSIA

I was in Malaysia in 1997 and again in 2003. My contacts were limited, so I have no authentic voice to speak about the mindset of Malaysian Indians. However, news clippings have given me the impression that as long as Hindus mind their own business, life is rather livable and even harmonious. However, if a Hindu is either in love with or married to a Muslim woman, he loses all rights and has to follow Sharia law from marriage to burial. The implication is that a Hindu cannot truly practice his or her own cultural values.

ISLAMIC REPUBLIC OF PAKISTAN

I visited numerous cities and most of the historical and religious sites in Pakistan during 2005. I was fortunate to have close encounters with Pakistani Hindus as well as Muslims. Hindus in Pakistan live under holocaust-like conditions, having no rights, respect, acceptance, safety, or protection under the law. The Hindu population has been reduced to a negligible number due to forced conversions, Waqf management of all temples and Gurudwaras, kidnapping and forced marriages of minor girls, and total absence of any protection. Pakistani Human Rights activists have verified these facts.

Ironically, many Pakistani Hindus have tried to immigrate to India but returned as they felt unwelcome and found no opportunities for work. It is amazing that Pakistan has the most significant Indian historical sites such as Harappa, Mohenjo-Daro, and Taxila, but Indians have been unable to visit or have been denied visas. In spite of the funds being provided by UNESCO, these sites are deteriorating rapidly due to a lack of maintenance. As these sites symbolize the apex of Hindu civilization, it seems Pakistanis would rather have them disappear.

DEMOCRATIC SOCIALIST REPUBLIC OF SRI LANKA

I visited Sri Lanka in 2004 during the height of civil strife and tension between Tamilians and Sinhalese. As a tourist, I did not notice or have the opportunity to learn much from personal encounters. However, news reports detailed the violence and mutual distrust. Unlike many countries, Sri Lanka does have an awareness of mental health issues and some services are available.

REPUBLIC OF TRINIDAD AND TOBAGO

I visited Trinidad and Tobago in December of 2007. Trinidad is known to be a reputable vacation paradise. Hindus have been under pressure since British colonization to convert to Christianity as cremation was illegal, and people with Christian names were given a priority in jobs and other forms of advancements. Politics of conversion aside, Hindus have been experiencing a great deal of domestic violence, marital and family disintegration, suicides, and alcoholism. Unlike Mauritius and Fiji, the Indian Diaspora is showing signs of chronic fatigue, and as a result, is losing its grounding in culture and heritage. Overall mental health has not become part of the society, and it is also not a national priority.

Indian Character through History

Every country's individual character is mirrored in its physical traits, culture, values and pursuits in life. These unique roots determine attitudes and direct the gestures and behavior of its people. While India never lost sight of the necessity of the material and intellectual dimension of life, she laid a particular emphasis on the moral and spiritual aspect. This spiritual dimension was non-existent in other countries until two thousand years ago, and then it developed only as an adjunct of religious dogmatism attached to a particular prophet and his set of religious tenets. Most religions like Judaism, Zoroastrianism, Christianity, Taoism, Buddhism, and Islam did not even come into existence until recently i.e. in the past 5000 years.

Spiritualism in India meant a dedication of one's life for perfect integration, self-realization, and oneness with the entire creation. Of all the countries of the world, India alone, with all the hypocrisy attributed to it by some foreign and even Indian writers, justifiably or otherwise, allows and even encourages search and research in the spiritual field as a worthy full-time goal in life. The Indian philosophical traditions, from the period of Vedas up to the modern time, present an amazing record of reflection on man's nature, interpersonal dynamics, and human destiny. Spinoza has correctly said that "the intellectual love of God" is a summary of Hindu philosophy. Hindu philosophy addresses psycho-socio-health-spiritual aspects of human beings in most relevant contexts ranging from personal growth, balancing family and social functioning as well as global harmony and prosperity.

Indian civilization is essentially spiritual. It is not religious but rooted in the highest form of humanity i.e. we all are one and the same and divine in nature. In Indian term, it is defined as dharma and not "religion." Dharma requires a continuous and sincere pursuit of the sacred over and above dogmas or any central control. People of India have a strong sense of individuality and at the same time, a sense "world is a family", enables them to think in terms of the universality and interdependence. Spread over a huge geographical area, `Indianity'–the essence of this polymorphous culture–is difficult to define. It acquires different postures and modes according to taste, attitudes, and mental sets of different groups and people united by an unspoken acceptance of certain constant social and cultural factors, such as the caste system, the belief in the cycle of successive lives, and sense of nationhood.

Every culture or society has ideals to which it is aspiring. The desired destination for Indian Hindus is Nirvana, i.e. total freedom from any and all attachments, karmic consequence, and emotional equanimity. The following are core concepts of Hindu character:

- Non-injury to any living thing or even to the plant as well as nature is the most essential aspect. From Vedic times to Buddha, Ashoka, and Mohandas Gandhi, all have been prophets of non-violence.
- Oneness with everything is the core belief of Hindus. This involves seeing self even in the smallest and most invisible creature and in friends and foes, each being an extension of one's own self.
- Relinquishing all desires, attachments, identities, and needing to control nothing is the Hindu approach to dealing with life.
- Non-reactivity as opposed to reactivity is the prescribed ideal for a Hindu. As a result, most of the Hindu practices such as meditation, yoga, fasting, and refraining from talking are all geared toward perfecting the management/homeo-stasis of the parasympathetic nervous system. One should be neutral in pleasure or pain, defeat or conquest, praise or criticism, or loss versus gain.
- Hindus subordinate actions to feelings, feelings to thought, thought to duty (dharma). And duty must be without any anticipations or expectations.
- Unlike other cultures, Hindus believe that from anger arises delusion, from delusion arises loss of memory, from

loss of memory arises the loss of pure reasoning, and from loss of pure reasoning arises destruction. In other words, unlike in Western culture, negative feelings are not just managed externally but must be addressed at its source of origin, i.e. desire.

- In Hindu psychology, the self is above intellect, "I", "mind", "five senses", "five motor organs," and the "five potentials". The Bhagavad Gita–based psycho-dynamics of emotional distress is defined by the following sequence: Abdominal-Anal-Genital Attachment → Desire → Anger → Confusion → Loss of Memory → Destruction of Intelligence → loss of ability to discriminate.

- Ego pathology is rooted in ignorance which binds us to obsession, habit conditioning, compulsions to act out of likes and dislikes, resulting in attachments, dependency, and addiction.

The roots of Indian spirituality were defined in the Vedic period, between 2000 and 500 BCE. During this period, the Vedas, the oldest scriptures of Hinduism, were composed.

Deterioration of Indian art, culture and thought started with the decline of the Gupta Period (500 AD), which is known as one of the "Golden Ages of India." Most of the energy and imagination of Indians was used up avoiding cultural adulteration, to protect the purity of their identity. They accomplished this by imposing extreme taboos and restrictions on intermingling with alien invaders. This attitude was further reinforced by various rituals, caste consciousness, and untouchability. This negative development of discrimination introduced divisiveness with long-term psychological, social, cognitive, and emotional consequences.

In medieval India, intellectual life was embedded in the teachings of Hindu and Muslim mystic saints. Most of them denounced idolatry, the caste system, and untouchability. They also condemned polytheism and believed in one god. The seventeenth century marked the apex of India's medieval feudal culture. At the beginning of the 18th century, the Mughal structure began to crumble. The British took full advantage of the weaknesses and follies of the Indian feudal rulers, Hindu and Muslim alike. Thus, another era of oppression started from 1757 onwards.

From the last decade of the medieval period to the beginning of modern times, Indian thought was in the grip of darkness. With no notable progress in the realm of thinking, political subjugation brought an all-around demoralization to Indians. The English education system in India, as introduced by British rule, to a great extent influenced the minds of educated men. They became great admirers of everything Western and in the course of time came to develop an inferiority complex and an attitude of contempt towards the great religious and cultural traditions of their own country. This was the first time, perhaps, that the Indian mind was thrown off balance.

Even the Muslim invasions and conquests had not produced a result of this kind. Indian scholars took great interest either in elaborating Western concepts or in having their ideas endorsed in Western literature. This "dependence proneness" or "follower syndrome" of Indians increased so much so that their own reasoning ability and creativity were blunted and stifled. The autonomy, effectiveness and productivity of Indian intellectuals became even feebler as they co-opted first Persian and later the Eurocentric/British way of looking at the self and the world.

As a result of the British-India encounter, Indians have developed a schizoid personality, best reflected in the famous

Hinduism warrants a very brief introduction. It is a bundle of six schools of psychological philosophies. It is evolutionary and perpetually goes through revisions, improvements and reforms. It has neither beginning nor an end. It is not a "one-size-fits-all". It promotes personal choices of psychological philosophies in appreciation of human nature, individual differences and personality make-up. Vedas are considered the central source and core of Hinduism. Hindu dharma presents the earliest systems of psychology, exploring human nature, personality, psycho-pathology, mental hygiene, treatment procedures as well as defining the role of positive psychology and spirituality as a value system. However, Euro-centric western psychology, is yet to fully recognize these contribution of Hinduism.

characterization of Indians by Thomas Babington Macaulay, who in 1835 introduced English education to India: "Their skin is still brown, but their mind is colonial." It seems safe to predict that this composite character will persist and that Indians will develop more of the excesses of modern, global culture, i.e. consumerism, loss of traditions, and the fragmentation of marriage and the nuclear family. It may be a sad journey for most of the Indian Diaspora since the countries they reside in are not equipped to deal with their particular mental health issues.

IDEAL IDENTITY: CORE VALUES

Every culture or society has aspirational ideals. The ultimate ideal for Hindu Indians is Nirvana, i.e. total freedom from all attachments, karmic consequence, and emotional rollercoaster.

In the article titled "Values of Indian and American Adolescents" Sundberg, Rohila, and Tyler (1970) compared values of Indian and American adolescents. They concluded that Indian lives center around family, with an emphasis on conformity, deference, and external control. Americans, on the other hand, emphasize sensuous enjoyment, religiosity, and sociability. At a visible level, Hindu behavior is determined by the following values:

- In the hierarchy of things, an individual is subordinate to the family, which is subordinate to the community, which, in turn, is subordinate to the country and all of them combined are guided by the ideal of Vasudhaiva Kutumbkam, i.e. the world is one family. Individuals are expected to make personal sacrifices such as women separating from their original family at marriage. Role-modeling renders all Indians – irrespective of their place in the family or society – responsible for adopting model ethics, morality, simplicity, wisdom, modesty and other virtues. As a result, the predominant mode of learning for Hindus is observational learning, rather than trial and error as is prevalent in the West.

- Obedience to the chronologically older person, anyone higher in the hierarchy, or to the person who is wise, scholarly, or has seniority is very acceptable and commonplace. By contrast, in the West, individuality and independence—even of a child—are nurtured.
- Self-worth is defined from inside and also based on one's sacrifices and character traits; unlike in the West, where its benchmarks are external such as appearance, height, sex appeal.
- Indians establish friendships for the sake of friendships, and it does not have to have to be based on factors such as sex, money, hobby, religion, or work.
- The Indian concept of space is very loose, almost to the point of being absent. As a result of their openness to space, they have no need for the concept of boundaries.

FAMILY DYNAMICS

The Indian family unit operates like a tribe. It is rooted in biological, hierarchical, predetermined roles and responsibilities, all living under one roof and bound by unconditional loyalty. Anything that threatens the family structure – modernization, change, entry, and exits from the unit – is viewed as a crisis. Separations, divorce, conversion, and marrying outside the tradition are all taboos. Any one member's failure, betrayal, lethargy, or ineptitude is capable of triggering dysfunction and disintegration of the family. The sons are the vehicles for the stability of the family and, therefore, every affair of their lives is micro-managed from birth until death. Daughters are brought up to get married and join their husbands' families, not only physically but emotionally and in terms of total loyalty. The sons' roles are complex, multiple and vital for the sustenance of the extended family. Even after getting married and having children, a man is expected to remain primarily a son, a brother, a cousin, and only then a father and husband. It's not hard to imagine that the burdens sons carry, and the sacrifices wives make are extraordinary, which is nothing less than cultural martyrdom.

Children are brought up tenderly, and every female in the family plays the maternal role. The queen mother in the family can be a mother or grandmother, who tends to be a benign dictator who keeps everyone in line. She has favorites: first born sons, grandsons, granddaughters, daughters, elderly, and only then daughter-in-laws. She makes sacrifices for everyone and does not usually have double standards, i.e. treating herself with special benefits or goodies. The grandfather tends to be on the sidelines and barely involved (see the later section, *The Elderly*).

The context of puppy love, dating, and living in common law arrangement is entirely different than the reality of the marriage. Healthy marriages—arranged or based on love— require honed, direct, open, blunt contractual understanding and agreeing about issues and values of sexual intercourse, parenting, handling in-laws, money matters, future directions and above all management of anger, fear, panic, worrying, jealousy, and other negative feelings." Love" is not good enough to guarantee happiness or harmony. Premarital counseling is a cost-effective measure to prevent unnecessary suffering and pain. Sex before marriage dilutes the sanctity of marriage. Dowry, domestic violence, and infidelity have no place in a healthy marriage. Happy marriages require two individuals feeling complete and then coming together rather than morbid clinging and dependency, or on expecting the other partner to make them feel good, secure or whole.

As overwhelming and stressful as this structure may seem, it has served Indians well. Compare the Indian family to those in any other culture or country and it uniquely stands out in terms of producing disciplined children, fewer or no delinquent adolescents, law-abiding citizens, and a culture that respects its adults like divinity. It has kept up the integrity of marriage and the sanctity of children being born and reared by both biological parents under the guidance of elders. The Indian family to date has the most evolved "cousin culture," i.e., no matter where they live or how long it has been since they've seen one another, the "cousins" maintain an intimate bond based on mutual friendship.

The traditional Indian family has gone through serious jolts and is undergoing dramatic changes not necessarily all positive. This has the potential risk of diluting everything Indian, from relational loyalties, passing cultural traditions on to the next generation, as well as the language, food, and music which are crucial to sustain one's unique identity. With the extinction of the

Indian extended family tradition, the death of India as we know her is inevitable. There is no escaping it. Change is inevitable but its haste and suddenness – due to urbanization, capitalism, materialism, consumerism, westernization, and hyper-individualistic orientation – is creating irreparable alienation, confusion, and socio-emotional pathology.

The decay of the Indian family is obvious and is visible through the increase in sibling rivalries, promiscuity, rape, alcoholism, vehicular homicides, and violence, all of which were previously exceptional behaviors. The impact of confusion and alienation will soon become apparent through an escalating trend of higher numbers of divorces, domestic violence, adultery, premarital pregnancies, depression, suicides, murders, and addictions.

The older generation is in crisis as well, feeling deaf, mute, dumb, blind and powerless due to the rapid loss of the familiar and no better replacement. The Diaspora has not come up with a viable solution. The elderly lack the skills to be autonomous. Furthermore, they fail to recognize the distress of the younger generation feeling sandwiched under the load of expectations from everybody. The elderly live by the old ideals of expecting the younger generation to be the "Shravan Kumar," the mythical Indian son who exhibited unparalleled devotion toward his parents, sacrificing everything personal. The days of collective sharing of resources, personal space, and extended family as meeting all needs of every member are gone forever. Families of the 21st century cannot continue to be the unconditional sanctuary for every generation and every significant other. In other words, there is no choice but to incorporate the values of self-dependency, individual responsibility, and timely planning.

The husband is in the epicenter of all family transactions by virtue of his being a son and being depended upon from guaranteeing security to problem solving. He is not at the top of the hierarchy but his multiple roles and obligations are vital due to his contributions and insurance value. Everybody wants a piece of him and his roles are so diverse that often he lives in a state of mini-breakdown (duress) and waits for bliss either through emigration, relocation, or if lucky, having parents who prefer their own autonomy, a rare occurrence.

The Indian husband feels that his first obligation and duty is to his parents and siblings and only then to his children and wife. One of the major marital conflicts in the Diaspora occurs when the wife is not able to or willing to follow the traditional protocol and instead demands attention, and solicits power to run her house her way. When the hierarchies are bypassed, the extended family fails to function. Most husbands operate on the basis of cultural assumptions that everybody, including their spouses, will surrender to the expected traditional roles and protocols. They do not feel the need to address these issues and often fail to renegotiate expectations. The Mahabharata of conflicts and power struggles becomes unmanageable when unresolved marital issues spill over into the lives of significant others and in-laws. This naiveté and assumptive attitude can potentially jeopardize the future of a marriage, and certainly peace of mind for years to come. There are no winners.

The Indian character trait of not openly verbalizing and negotiating expectations with parents, spouses, significant others and family relatives, friends, guests and visitors often plays havoc with lasting consequences. Indians, male or female, characteristically operate on assumptions borrowed from traditions and culture. They anticipate as well as expect that others will understand them. This pattern is deeply rooted in the Indian personality because of the preference to avoid confrontation at any cost, and also not to be open with their agendas and ulterior motives. This character defect is not malicious, but simply a learned behavior to take the easy way out from any possibility of confrontation.

Another major stressor Indian husbands experience is rooted in their family expectations as well their self-imposed need to ensure the settling of their siblings. This role revolves around financially providing for their education, seeking employment, and even negotiating their marriage. This sacrifice often tends to be one-sided, due to the idealistic need to be a positive role model and to prove his loyalty while expecting parental admiration. Wives notice this parasitic or abusive pattern, but the husbands lack skills to question or confront their siblings. Wives' protests prove futile, often resulting in anger and marital conflicts as husbands expect them to surrender and acquiesce. The complaining does not stop, in spite of its futility. Typically, the intention is to protect the nuclear family's financial resources; the husband should "wise up," see the game, and renegotiate the boundaries. Here again the expected loyalty to siblings

Individuals consult psychologists not just for mental illnesses but often to improve the quality of their "being," relationships, and to feel positive and live productive lives. These life goals are often sabotaged and complicated, mainly because people have no clear definition and act in a hit and miss fashion. Happiness is possible only when one has conceptual clarity, wakes up with a purpose, and then makes it happen. Happiness primarily is contentment, acceptance of life, living in the moment, being Satvik, integrating spirituality, and balancing it with sensory pleasures. The importance of money is oversold. Intimacy, praying, playing, giving, simplicity, laughing, and being in the moment do not cost money. Self-imposed conditions like "bigger", "longer", "higher, "more", "greater", better" based on comparison with others and competitiveness are an irreversible road to misery.

becomes a genuine source of abuse, misuse, and aggravation and impacts negatively on the marriage.

Also, Indian husbands see their paternal families and all their clan members as superior to the in-laws' family while the wife's family is considered lower in the hierarchy. Their expected behavior is to shower the husband's family with gifts, recognition, and self-sacrifice. In recent times, Indian wives have become aware of these dynamics and desire equality and freedom from traditional expectations. However, in the interim, it remains a significant source of martial conflict. The essential dynamics of Indian husbands revolves around meeting complex unspoken expectations of parents, siblings, spouses, children, and the extended family.

As a consequence his separation, differentiation, individuation, and in essence being himself is not an option, at least during Grihastha phase of life. In this context, it is easy to understand that assertiveness, decisiveness, taking charge, confronting expectations, and communicating clearly are all very difficult for him. His fear is that the balance will be disturbed; creating a ripple in the status quo that will leave him too paralyzed to regain control. Husbands fear exposure and find safety in being private, subtle, and indirect, even at the cost of losing credibility and creating a negative image. Indian wives feel dismissed and perceived as incompetent adults by their husbands. They often complain that their husbands do not understand their side, or advocate for them, and fail to support their emotional needs. This interplay exposes the conflicts, leading to vulnerability and potential confrontation. This behavioral pattern of passivity is the most common defense mechanism utilized to shield oneself from any threat, both internal and external.

EMOTIONAL BLACKMAIL

Indian husbands tend to be seen by their spouses as emotional scammers due to them acting as cultural robots, being emotionally apathetic and self-absorbed. On the other hand, in their other roles as sons, siblings, and fathers, they are devoted to perfection. In the husband role, men are obsessed with control, but at the same time do not openly discuss their agendas or feelings. They keep their wives busy by controlling their incomes, pressuring them to live "simply," i.e. by expecting them not to be consumers, buy luxury items, finance purely emotional traveling (homesick) to India, and pressuring them not to send money to their parents or siblings. Lots of marital intimacy is lost due to struggles over money, fun, leisure time activities, and savings. In many marriages, husbands fail to define the financial situation realistically. They remain rooted in unconscious insecurities and overcompensate by hoarding. Anecdotally, women are known to complain that men lack intimacy, emotional responsiveness and tend to be self-absorbed. Self-absorption is a rather pervasive Indian personality trait. Husbands often miss, ignore, or dismiss wives' clues, verbalizations, emotions, and gestures as stressors. When the wife's protests becomes very overt, she is perceived as adversarial, unreasonable, demanding and responsible for ruining the marriage. When the husband's passivity becomes blatant and intolerable, the wife blames the husband for the cause of her depression and ruining the marriage. The gender psychology is different and often misunderstood universally. As a result, male and female relationships, especially in marriage often tend to be conflicted. Marriage therapists observe this phenomenon of pervasive dissatisfaction amongst spouses, causing unwarranted physical and emotional consequences involving finances, children, and intimacy.

TRISHANKU SYNDROME

The Indian husband's state of mind can be metaphorically summarized as *Trishanku*–neither here nor there and perpetually in limbo. The phrase "Trishanku's heaven" is used widely in India to describe such situations/dilemmas faced in real life.

Trishanku is a character from the ancient Hindu literary tradition, and the phrase describes a middle-ground or a compromise between goals or desires and the current state. Trishanku is suspended in his own heaven as a compromise between the Earth that he belonged to and the heaven that he sought. He is hanging in heaven upside down.

MASTER OF DEFENSIVENESS

Indian husbands more often than not will go to any length to avoid being confronted, even if constructively, because the realization of being imperfect, wrong, or needing to change is just too overwhelming. Their rigidity and resistance are rooted in the lack of ability to identify and manage their own feelings as well as those of significant others. Regardless of who he interacts with, the man remains hyper focused on tasks and goals but not on emotional and interpersonal process. He will resist or even avoid to seek professional help regardless of the damage to their profession, family and relations.

As a psychologist, I have seen many marriages end in divorce even when the wife underwent treatment and made changes, wrote letters sharing very openly and constructively, and took most of the blame. In these instances, it is common for the husband never to respond, join therapy, or seek help for himself. Such defensiveness in the Indian character goes beyond husband-hood and is endemic in politicians, professionals, police, the court system, and all institutions.

SELF-ABSORPTION

Taking things for granted comes naturally to Indians as it spares them from the responsibility to keep updating and renegotiating relationships whether in business, marriage or friendships. This trait of hyper-focusing on their needs, agendas, and goals tends to sabotage the interactive process. As opposed to Westerners, Indians tend not to provide positive reinforcements and feedback due to the belief system that it should be a given. Unlike Americans, Indians do not have adequate awareness as to the value of positive reinforcement tools such as rewards, tokens, or incentive options in their repertoire. Unspoken expectations tend to determine interpersonal transactions with risky consequences. By and large this is a rather pervasive Indian personality trait. When a wife's behavior becomes very overt or vocal, she is shunned for being aggressive and causing shame to the family.

MALES AND HUSBANDS: CASE STUDIES

IRONY OF VENGEANCE

This case involved an Indian professional who was young, and very successful but depressed. His wife was also a professional and very successful. They had chronic and very serious marital incompatibilities partly because they both came from different socio-economic classes. He saw his wife as wasteful, immature and aggressive. She perceived him as cheap, thrifty, and money-obsessed with no regard for feelings and fun.

They never sought professional help as they did not want exposure. The relationship ended with the wife killing herself and her only child so that he could collect a large insurance settlement.

Outstanding features of this case point out:

- Marital power struggles were symbolic of their incompatibilities, class differences and lack of awareness and openness to seek professional help.
- The wife most likely had serious emotional problems and marriage was the perfect stage to act out her childhood conflicts involving her parents, etc.
- Either of the spouses could have gone for individual counseling and broken the vicious cycle that lead to murder-suicide.
- Both spouses got hooked into the money obsession and forgot that other powerful emotions were churning and also needed to be addressed.
- Feelings, if not dealt with, tend to spill over either in terms of accident proneness, physical illness or outright mental illness.
- The passive-aggressive pattern is very Indian. M. Gandhi defeated the British with this maneuver. However, in relationships, it is very damaging

THE IVY LEAGUE GRADUATE

Manohar was a 32-year-old single male, Ivy League graduate, and was employed in the hedge fund industry. He had a Ph.D. in Financial Engineering. His father died when he was 22, and his mother lived in India. His grandfather died at age 42 from alcoholism. His mother was known to be chronically dissatisfied with her life because she had given up her education and ambitions due to marriage at age 18. The patient revealed that his childhood was full of embarrassment and difficulties because of his father's alcoholism, power struggles between his father and grandfather, and marital arguments.

He consulted me for having impulsively resigned from his high paying job following an episode of extreme rage, acting out, confusion, paranoia, and delusional behavior toward his coworker. He had ended up in a psychiatric hospital.

Outstanding features of this case point out:

- He suffered from a bipolar mood disorder that triggered an episode resulting in delusional behavior and impulsive resignation i.e. impaired judgment.
- He was neither properly diagnosed nor complying with the medication, counseling, required lifestyle changes and practice of yoga for self-help.
- His unresolved chronic childhood dependency issues, rooted in his relationship conflicts with parents, were unmet in spite of his being 32 years old.
- His brilliance and success provided him intellectual cover but no resolution of his ambivalence toward his mother, fear of being on his own and avoidance of getting married and settling down.
- Unresolved feelings, relationship conflicts, and childhood traumas tend to linger on indefinitely unless addressed in psychotherapy.

WIVES

The Indian wife is the person primarily responsible for passing on Indian values to future generations. She not only plays the role of a wife, but she is a mother, sister, daughter-in-law, and a friend, who for ages has been given the responsibility of preserving the religious and cultural values of India and preserving the "Indian-ness" in children. Although all the members of the family share the responsibility of protecting Indian values from becoming distorted in the shadow of modern beliefs, it is the women of the house who most embody these responsibilities.

The status of Indian wives varies depending upon the husband's order of birth, his success and contribution to the extended family, the size of the family, expectations of the significant others, and how many female siblings are still unmarried and living at home.

In the scheme of things, the husband's mother has queen status, the husband's sisters stand second, and the Indian wife comes in third. In other words, wives live in an "on hold" status, like a woman waiting for recognition, reprieve, peace of mind, and some sanity. A New Jersey housewife married for 20 years summarizes her feelings as follows:

> *"After going through all possible psychological changes and different family circumstances, I realized in the end that I am still not in the position to distinguish my duties to myself and my duties towards the family. I am torn apart between trying to find my own individuality and my responsibilities and duties dictated to me by society and parents. Being told since childhood that I should find the happiness in 'giving' to the family, I never developed my ability to receive or accept any natural feelings, this includes sexual pleasure also."*

A wife's background determines her status and place. Some factors include whether she comes from an influential/rich family, what level of education she has completed, whether she came with an adequate dowry, and whether her parents went out of their way to accommodate the husband's family. The wife's status is also defined by her ability to be a team player, her competence in mediating or not getting involved in power struggles, and her proficiency as a house cleaner/cook/caretaker of elderly family members. In Indian society, the biggest impact of feminism has been on women in the spousal role asserting their individuality based on Western, particularly American, expectations.

The wife's most important allies are her mother-in-law and sister(s)-in-law. The wife of the oldest son is highest in the pecking order. It is important to note that the couple's intimacy and sexual needs are secondary to the business of taking care of the family. In other words, wives probably have the same amount of stress, exhaustion, and challenges as the husbands have in their multiple roles as sons, siblings, fathers and providers of the clan. While the husband can walk away to work or mingle with friends, wives have fewer social outlets. Thus, mood shifts, depression, and psychosomatic disorders are common.

After marriage, the bride traditionally moves to her husband's house, leaving behind her parental house and the memories of her childhood to lead an entirely new and different life. This is the biggest sacrifice she makes in her life, to compromise personal dreams and desires. Perhaps more than other cultures, the emotion of sacrifice is recognized and revered. Indian brides are famous for demonstrating the values of forgiveness and sacrificing for the benefit of the family.

The following are characteristics that are common to most wives, but especially to Indian wives:

- *Loyalty to husband:* An Indian wife sustains a deep loyalty with or without love for her husband. This stems from tradition, religion, and upbringing and is not always feeling-based.

- *Home is her castle:* In the role of a wife, an Indian woman is fully cognizant of the necessity, importance and the long-term impact as to the dynamics of home culture. Everyone's mental health depends upon it as to how harmonious and peaceful the home base is.

- *Commitment to tradition and continuity of culture:* In the wife's role, she is obligated, empowered and privileged to enrich the family with the proper holistic nourishment, promoting the pursuit of spirituality and keeping the family glued. She is unmistakably the builder and protector of Indian tradition.

- *Honoring family customs:* She follows the family customs, keeps the traditions, and emerges as the empowered specialist as the facilitator of the rituals and samskaras.

- *Readiness for Marriage:* The Indian wife grows up with full awareness since childhood as to her role as a wife. She typically adopts herself to her husband, his family and their traditions, and to whatever circumstances life thrusts upon her. Personal individuality and the need for boundaries are not viewed as significant. Traditionally it worked rather well.

However, a wife's role now has become very stressful and the pressures to work, rear children, run the household and also to care for significant others of her own and husband's side of the family.

WIVES: CASE STUDIES

THE CONSERVATIVE BRAHMAN

Triveni was an India-born 48-year-old female, married to a very conservative Indian whose family lived in London, UK. He was raised there. She consulted me initially for nervousness, excessive fears, and an inability to function in her roles as a wife and an adult. She was perpetually sad, ready to cry and very low on confidence and self-esteem. She was unable to enjoy anything and was extremely insecure. Her background included a history of family mental illness. She had undergone numerous psychiatric treatments as well as counseling, but with no improvement or any hope for anything ever to change.

She often reported anticipating failure, helplessness, confusion, and doom and gloom. The rare occasions she felt any reprieve was when her husband was away from home, or she traveled to India. She saw her husband as loud, bossy, aggressive, controlling, critical, and disapproving and felt that she could never please him. She felt abandoned by her husband and blamed him for making her feel insecure and nervous. She had had three mental breakdowns prior to seeing me.

My interviews with the husband revealed that in spite of having lived in England and now in the USA, he was stuck in his conservative, Brahamanic ways and was excessively obsessive, and fixated on his wife. He participated in the mutual suffering as if that was the only game in town. He would force her to come for therapy, but at the same time, was never convinced that changes by him could improve the culture of his home or that he would benefit from it. No matter what suggestions were made, he was unable to let go of the past and often blamed her for not telling him before the marriage that she had a family history of mental problems. He lacked any and all empathy for his wife and locked her in a role of being "dishonest, playing negative games, and being lazy." He never stopped comparing her with other women or trying to prove she was incompetent.

Outstanding features of this case point out:

- Her distress was internal due to family history and her own mental illness, but her husband used her as a scapegoat due to his pent-up rage and need to avoid focus on self. This was a major factor in her repeated hospitalizations and chronic melancholia.
- Her husband needed counseling but was not open or willing. He preferred for his wife to be the designated mental patient in the family. The husband's inability to live in the "here and now," and to relinquish his family of origin in England was a maneuver to avoid growing up and let go of his bitterness.
- The wife had no resources or support system to be on her own and, so, there was no hope for the family/marriage system to change.

THE UNHAPPY WIFE

Ganga was a 23-year-old married woman with no children, who was born in Surat, and at age 20 came to the U.S. to join her husband. She lived in the U.S. with her husband, both in-laws, and a sister-in-law who was mentally handicapped. While cooking, cleaning, and taking care of the in-laws, she also held a job. Her husband was the only son, highly educated, a professional, and a strict vegetarian.

She came to see me because of episodes of depression with suicidal thoughts, pervasive dissatisfaction, crying, feeling fed up with her life, having difficulty functioning in the wife role, inability to sleep, and overreacting to even small irritations. She repeatedly injured herself by peeling her skin.

She was fearful of becoming pregnant because she did not want the child to be trapped. She had lost all interest in living. She did not want to live with her husband, but she did not want to abandon him either, as he was a very caring husband. He just could not establish boundaries between himself and his mother. She was regretful of ever having married in the first place.

Once, she had even returned to India to distance herself from her in-laws. She described her mother-in-law as self-absorbed, never satisfied, super religious, unhappy with her own husband, and obsessing with her son in terms of all her expectations being met by him. Her world revolved around her son. She had many health problems and faked her dependence to the extreme.

The suffering was absolutely unnecessary. The causes of suffering in this situation were the following: the mother-in-law did not want to accept the daughter-in-law or any change in the household culture, which was required because of her marriage. The more she felt dependent, the more she feared losing control over her son. Her concept of loyalty was morbid, and she chose sadistic ways to exercise her control. The son was naïve about his mother's symbiotic relationship with him and failed to renegotiate his husband role with his mother. He was unwilling to take on an adult and husband role due to cultural guilt and an unspoken oath of blind loyalty to his parents.

THE SHOPLIFTER

Prema was middle-aged, born and raised in India, the youngest of five siblings, and had her degree in microbiology. She came to the U.S. in 1984, got married in 1985 and had a daughter. When I saw her, she had been married for 19 years and was employed in the food and beverage industry. Her husband also had a college degree and an outstanding job.

She came to see me because she was being charged for repeated shoplifting offenses. She wanted help only to avoid jail. She had no interest in understanding her behavior or managing her shoplifting compulsion. She thought paying a fee for the services and the report was a waste. In addition, she wanted nobody else to be involved. As a result, it was next to impossible to schedule appointments with her.

Her secretiveness, denial of reality, resisting to pay for

services, and difficulty in communicating on the phone, made it very difficult for me to help her. As she was non-compliant, I have no idea as to her fate.

Outstanding features of this case point out:

- Her biggest handicap was her inability to trust and relinquish control.
- She was in denial of the nature of her problem which had to do with impulse disorder, loss of control and ambivalence about attention seeking.
- She was also unconsciously punishing her husband by being passive aggressive.
- She had extreme obsessive preoccupation and conflict regarding money. She had no separate funds except her marital bank accounts.

THE BREADWINNER

Anita was a 32-year-old, college educated, Brahman, conservative female married to a Lucknow, India-born Non-Resident Indian (NRI). The marriage took place during a brief visit by her husband to India. After the marriage, she stayed with her in-laws in the U.S. Her husband was extremely attached (symbiotic) to his father and behaved like a little boy. His elder sister was dictatorial and the decision-maker.

Anita developed depression after six months of living with the joint family. Instead of the family respecting their privacy and encouraging autonomy, they did just the opposite. During this process, the husband reacted by being violent and abusive to his wife who had no family or friends in the U.S. She was physically abused by her in-laws and husband, including being locked out of the house.

She was the breadwinner of the household. She became pregnant which only worsened the situation. Her husband was emotionally dependent on his family-of-origin while financially dependent on his wife. Following prolonged violence, she moved, to live on her own, with her infant daughter. Her husband joined her but spent most of his time with his father and sister. He was unable to hold a job, became depressed, and grew increasingly more dependent (clinging). He was not able to function in the role of a husband or a father due to his extremely dependent personality. In spite of being mistreated by her brother and sister-in-law during her childhood in India, she had no prior history of any emotional or interpersonal problems.

She came to see me because of severe depression, violent outbursts, and loss of appetite, inability to function at work, insomnia, pervasive conflicts with her in-laws, and an inability to cope with her husband's personality dysfunction. She had acted out dangerously and destructively. She felt powerless and despondent but due to cultural factors was neither open to separation nor returning to India. She initially was against her husband seeking professional help or medication. She was not open to seeking help. The conflicts went on for many years, with prolonged suffering, mutual violence, and repeated involvement of the police and the legal institution.

Outstanding features of this case point out:
- It was an arranged marriage, carried out on short notice, and matching was based on caste, class, and the husband being in the U.S. She had the expectation that the marriage would meet all her emotional needs. She would be at her best in running her household, and above all, would finally become free from the demands of her extended family.
- Her husband suffered from borderline personality disorder. His dependency was enabled and exploited by his parents and sister. The existence of mental problems was ignored.
- They never expected, encouraged, or promoted autonomy or mutually productive adult roles and instead enabled incompetence and infantile dependence. Above all, the entire family became united under the pretense of feeling victimized. Their hostility towards Anita was unconscious and an exercise in controlling behavior.
- They were not open to feedback or professional help. They solved all their problems by blaming the victim and seeing

their son as the ultimate victim. The husband's core conflict revolved around not being able to separate and adequately function in his roles as son, brother, husband, father, and ultimately as an adult in the community.

The patient was exhausted with an overload of responsibility, pervasive sabotage by her in-laws, having complete financial responsibility for the household and what appeared to be an absolutely hopeless future. Her aggression was a survival mechanism representing her despondence, feeling trapped and rendered helpless.

CHILDREN

Indian parents do not see their children as equals but at the bottom of the totem pole. This is not because they see children as unimportant, but because the social structure of Indian society is hierarchical. This is not seen as a negative but conducive for children to evolve, learn observationally, grow, accomplish, look up to their elders, and earn their medals. Particularly in Hindus, the belief is that the "ego," "I," "me," and "mine" must be depleted or suspended as a prerequisite to becoming wise, learned, and mature. That is one of the reasons children are not expected to have an ego or even an illusion that they are unique, special, or entitled to extraordinary privileges.

Children are provided for, protected, inspired, and loved dearly. This expression of love is less verbal than in the West. Indian parents tend not to be verbose, repetitive, or go overboard in letting the child know he is loved. It's not the giving of cakes, sneakers, clothes, gifts, or compliments which are equated with love, but rather the family sharing, mutual sacrifices of personal comforts, soft tone of voice, tender looks, inspiration, and exposure to opportunities.

Children of the Indian Diaspora tend to have a clear awareness of their home culture over the mainstream majority culture. They are exposed to the differences in school, at playgrounds, and their interactions with their peers. By and large, most youngsters are comfortable with this duality and rarely display any inferiority about being Indian. However, they are aware of being different, not only in terms of physical appearance, but in their awareness that their families expect them to achieve, accomplish, and surpass others. They complain of missing out on some of the liberties and fun that their peers have. However, by and large they conform to the family discipline and expectations. They also tend to have a rather unique "cousin culture," which empowers them regardless of where their cousins, extended family, or fellow Diasporans reside. The participation in the "cousin network" helps them laugh and share the paradoxes of life in cultural dissonance, and also allows them to give and receive mentoring and counseling.

I have counseled numerous families. I also helped conduct a summer camp for Indian children, during which I asked them individually and in groups to discuss common issues. Although many of the themes outlined below are particularly relevant for U.S. Diaspora families, they likely echo issues experienced by Diaspora families worldwide.

- Indian children often complain that their parents micro-manage their behavior and that all of their time is watched, supervised, and controlled. This extreme overprotectiveness makes children yearn to be free but at the same time afraid of venturing too far. I have seen many adolescents, school and college students alike; have a mental breakdown over having to be on their own, even while living in college dormitories.
- Indian parents tend to raise the bar every time a child is successful instead of celebrating the accomplishment.
- Indian parents' communication styles tend to be "preachy" or sermonizing and make repeated references as to "how it was back in the old days." This is a subtle expectation game Indian parents play that makes children feel put down, ashamed and confused as to their cultural identity.
- Children are not encouraged to express opinions and share feelings. These feelings, both repressed and suppressed, can

have dire consequences from depression to suicide.

- Indian parents lack sensitivity as to the importance of peer interaction, opportunity for trial and error, exposure to experiences outside of Indian culture, and peer pressure. Children are expected to be home immediately after school. Even at home, downtime is discouraged, and homework and studying, learning and expanding the information base is emphasized above all else.

- The Indian belief is that the first 25 years of our lives are to build character, acquire education, learn etiquette, and empower oneself with extraordinary achievement whether in spelling bees, tennis championships or other activities. This belief that energy is limited and has to be channeled very strictly can cause a great deal of stress among children.

- In the U.S., Indian parents do not trust the American style of "hanging out," i.e. purposeless socializing or congregating in the street or malls. It is seen as potentially troublesome and risky as well as a sheer waste of time. They do not see any good or social value in spending time without a specific purpose, i.e. education, information-gathering, or achieving excellence. Sports, athletics, or social activities including hobbies are viewed as distractions.

- Parents tend to dictate children's choices regarding the direction of education and what should be their profession. They are insensitive to the individuality or personal choices of the child. This is because Indians, for the most part, are thinking that the goal of education should be attaining both status and money. Their children may resent being coerced into becoming a doctor or a lawyer. They are essentially given prepackaged options.

- Children frequently report that they do not know whom to talk to about their feelings or emotions. They end up following the cultural duty and by doing so, sublimating or repressing their feelings. As their parents also avoid dealing with their feelings, they pass on this same pattern to their children. Talking to a psychologist is not familiar and also not trusted with personal or family matters. Straight A's and academic success are used by parents to obfuscate the emotional issues or needs of their children. .

- During the camp I alluded to above, children expressed significant anxiety about sex-related issues. They showed awareness that it was a forbidden issue.

- Psychological testing of the children in the camp revealed that they saw their mothers as somewhat assertive and their fathers as "smaller" and effeminate.

- Most children in the camp expressed the need for attention, closeness, and recognition. Regardless of their plans for the future, they all felt they needed to be "the best," i.e. stand out academically and professionally.

- Indian girls have a hard time because they are "not being allowed to talk about boys at home." They manifest their anger by yelling at others in the family or by withdrawing.

- As they mature and enter adulthood, youth often feel resentful that they are expected to have an arranged marriage as opposed to a relationship 'merely' for love. Although arranged marriages are fast disappearing in the Indian Diaspora, the practice reflects the traditional Hindu view that marriage is supposed to serve more of a social and family function than a strictly individual one. The core belief is responsibility first, love and sex later.

CHILDREN: CASE STUDIES

HOMICIDAL AT AGE SIX

A 6-year-old Gujarati girl was referred to me because she attempted to drown her four-year-old brother in the tub. Her parents' elder brother, his wife, and two children had come from India to live with them. The parents were very loving and caring and lived in a two-bedroom apartment in New Jersey. The family was happy and well-adjusted until the great uncle's family came to live with them.

As culture dictates, the great uncle and his family were

given priority. As a result, the girl lost her bedroom as well as her personal space. Not having a sympathetic ear, she resorted to protesting via hostile behavior. Once the parents were shown the dynamics and advised to stop alienating the girl, everything went back to normal.

Outstanding feature of this case point out:

- Indians in India (IIN) are very comfortable in sharing space and sacrificing their personal comfort to accommodate relatives, seniors, and significant others. However, the same Indian child born or raised in the U.S. cannot conceptualize not having his or her own space.
- Indian children born or brought up in Western cultures tend to have a very clear sense of personal space, boundaries, individuality, and mutual privacy.
- Unlike in India due to the context of the extended family culture, the children brought up in Western cultures tend to react to changes in their personal or family lives akin to a traumatic experience.

UNFOCUSED CHILD

Anil was an 11-year-old U.S. born fifth grader. His parents were Gujarat born immigrants living in Pennsylvania. They were concerned about his behavioral problems. He displayed an inability to accept structure and limitations, became easily excited, was very irritable, and lacked motivation. He was very demanding and acted immaturely. He displayed impulsivity and lacked focus. He was fearful of going to school and interacting with peers. The school's evaluation indicated an average IQ and a friendly, talkative, student with symptoms of restlessness.

The family dynamics was complicated by Anil feeling that his father did not interact or help him with his homework. He saw his father as always being busy and having too high of expectations for his grades. His mother's cooking was very spicy which he did not like. Anil felt that nobody understood him.

Diagnostically he suffered from Attention Deficit Disorder and parent-child relational problems.

Outstanding features of the case point out:

- The family culture was conventional; expectations were high but without the acceptance of Anil's handicap and stress.
- The family did not positively reinforce his individuality.
- His father micro-managed his life from his food preferences to his style of haircut.
- His exposure to mainstream society was limited to the interactions he had while in school.

THE ELDERLY

Indian family dynamics operate on the principles of loyalty, hierarchy, mutual dependence, and duty-over-feelings. Sacrifice over individual desires keeps the elderly in a meaningful structure and a purposeful mindset. Traditionally, the elderly have been known not to fear death, seek vanity, live in denial or exhibit any significant mental illness. Elderly men remain more detached to domestic affairs while elderly women take on the role of mediating with the outside world or getting into maternal-type roles "for the younger generation."

The role of the elderly in the Indian family dynamic is best understood in the context of the Hindu concept of the four phases of life, which will be discussed later in this book. In this worldview, the elderly male is in the Vanaprastha phase, and is expected to begin to disengage from the rat race and family entanglements, choosing instead to intensify subordination of his energy into spiritual pursuits and serving the larger society.

Some other observations:

- It is an unspoken contract that the Indian elderly expect to depend on the younger generation for their needs. The younger generation is obligated to pay their dues and prove their respect and loyalty to elder family members.
- Sons, especially, the older ones are expected to be the primary family caretakers.
- Typically Indian elderly live a minimalist life, sublimating

their energies toward religious and spiritual practices. However, their emotional neediness does not dissipate.

- The elderly use their hierarchical power as the conscience, super ego, and a reminder of the moral duties of everyone to keep the family integrated, undivided, and respected in the community.

ELDERLY: CASE STUDIES

RETIRED AND AIMLESS

Vijay was a 70 year-old, Bombay-born Maharashtrian who was married and had four sons. He was financially very successful, had retired from his job, and was continuing his real estate investments. He had no support system other than an extended in-law family. He was compelled to undergo counseling by his wife who was unable to tolerate his drinking habits. His children were unable to relate to him and felt resentment. His life revolved around his real estate, wife, and children.

Diagnostically he was depressed, had marital problems, parent-child issues, and alcohol dependence.

Outstanding features of this case point out:
- Vijay was a very kind individual but was unable to cope with changes in routine and a new phase of life.
- He lived for his family, without a life of his own, and when his family achieved independence, he was lost.
- The more he tried to cling to the family, the more rejected he felt. He used alcohol to cope with his "pity party" and abandonment issues.
- He had no insight into his emotional neediness and its negative impact on significant others
- He rationalized his drinking by blaming it on his wife's preferring her mother and brother over him.

CROWDED BUT LONELY

Sonpal was an 85-year-old retired widower, who came to the U.S.A. to be with his three sons and grandchildren. When he arrived, only one of his children hosted him while his other sons refused to communicate. He suffered severe depression and other health problems and he was unable to overcome the humiliation and abandonment he felt by his two sons.

Diagnostically he suffered from major depression, phase of life problems, and parent-child problems.

Outstanding features of this case point out:
- The traditional expectation of an extended family being united and displaying respect for him was the primary cause of his depression.
- Intergenerational conflicts among his significant others were pervasive. Additionally there was no willingness or openness to confront the issues. As a result, he felt even more neglected, alienated, and pitiful.
- Immigration was intended to unite the family, but it turned out to be painful with the awareness that all his children and their families are not close to each other. Immigration is not a guarantee for a family to live happily ever after.
- Families need to negotiate openly about arrangements and expectations whenever relatives or guests come to live with them or even visit temporarily.

PARENTING IN THE DIASPORA

Raising Indian children in India is different from raising Indian children in countries with different cultures, values, and lifestyles. Raising Diaspora children often involves a clash between the culture of host countries and traditional Indian values.

In the U.S. and Europe, this means a clash between Western values and lifestyle versus with Eastern values and lifestyle. The former emphasizes individuality, consumerism, and autonomy while the latter idealizes family loyalty, minimalism, and mutual dependence. In non-Western countries, the cultural clash takes different forms.

Whatever the country they reside in, all Indian Diaspora parents are influenced by the Hindu perspective on the meaning of parenting. Simply put, Hindus see the parents' role as facilitating the child's growth, helping them learn good habits and concepts, and providing a means of helping children grow up to be productive and responsible world citizens. They don't view the child as "theirs," but as given to them in trust for the good of the whole society. They also view themselves as the children's first teacher (guru), an awesome responsibility especially for those whose practice of Hinduism is a little thin.

It is safe to conclude that the cultural difference between Indian parents and their children is a major and pervasive source of stress, especially in the U.S. and other developed countries. Resolutions and breakthroughs are very difficult to achieve since children raised in the Diaspora have an awareness of their own stress, expectation overload, parental rigidity, and emotional-interactive inaccessibility. Parents do not see their children as emotional beings having their own unique stresses and challenges. This is because in the USA and other developed countries, the Indian Diaspora arrived about four decades ago and has failed to recognize the high incidence of mental illness. However, ethnic newspapers have been reporting a great deal of news regarding Indians' emotional problems and criminal behavior. In less affluent countries, challenges such as racial strife, political barriers, poverty, violence, and addiction most likely result in higher incidences of mental illness. However, this is difficult to confirm as relatively little research has been done.

STRATEGIES FOR EFFECTIVE PARENTING

Especially in the complexity of the 21st century, parenting is challenging regardless of background, ethnicity, religion, or socioeconomic status. Traditional parenting was learned and practiced as a cultural and religious role modeling. The "trial and error" approach was not very acceptable to Indians. However, with the popularity of modern psychology, worldwide exposure via media, and easy international traveling or living in foreign cultures, a great deal of confusion has prevailed. The pressure on parents to integrate psychologists' recommendations as well as some of the values and norms of traditional and modern perspectives has exacerbated the situation. As children's expectations have changed, they show a clear awareness of cross-cultural and cross-religious differences. What follows is a mix of my observations and opinions I've expressed to parents:

- Children do well when they are living in an environment with certainty, predictability, and continuity. Honesty in sharing of feelings and behavioral transparency can go a long way.

- Children have feelings that need to be listened to, acknowledged, and that they should be encouraged to share and express. One should not wait for a crisis, acting out, or legal entanglements to realize the power of feelings. They should be respected rather than judged or discouraged.

- Children may be the lowest in the hierarchy, but their needs for privacy, personal space, personal preferences, likes, and dislikes are important, and they should be allowed experimentation within certain boundaries.

- Relatives and religion should not be imposed on children. Their interest and involvement should be facilitated gently, gradually and with a lot of patience. They may rebel during adolescence but by their thirties they almost always return to their roots. Having patience is the best way to cope.

- Regardless of the strengths of the Indian culture, one should not think that it is the perfect culture. Children should be raised with an appreciation of the "best of both worlds."

- There is nothing wrong with having clear moral/social standards and expectations. For example it is perfectly okay to convey to children that engaging in alcohol/drug abuse, irresponsible sex, and making children without ensuring proper and durable parenting are not grey areas open to experimentation or compromise.

- Do not worry if your children are not your clones or if they confront you with your personal inconsistencies and hypocrisies. Unlike in India, parenting involves two-way street of sharing. Let your children help you grow.

- Do not obsess with children. Stop micromanaging and living for them. Be a husband or wife, be socially active, have hobbies and a life apart from them. Help them manage their own stress rather than feeling like you have to manage it for them.

- Promote a psychological sense of separation, individuation, and autonomy in your children. It will make them resilient and better able to face adversity. Your second role, as they transition from childhood to adulthood, is to "prepare them for the jungle" and become their teacher. In this way you can help them to be powerful, efficient adults and decision-makers. Their eventual autonomy does not mean disloyalty or disrespect to you.

- Leave them alone in their room or personal space; let them decorate it the way they want. Do not go in the room unless it's a health hazard, filthy beyond belief or some crime is being committed. I tell parents to think that their children's rooms are like foreign countries: you can't go there unless you have a visa. It may seem too simple, but your children will respect you if you let them be free to be in their own space.

- Do not dictate their ultimate choice of profession based on your insecurities or need for status. Chances are they will follow you in any case and, at worst, find their own way.

- Remember the only crises in life are death, disaster, fire, or cancer. The rest of the problems are just mere passing events. Promoting children's excellence is admirable, but not at the cost of their happiness, mental well-being, and health. Nothing is worth having a psychotic breakdown or committing suicide. Then you will really have a crisis.

- Imitating Western parenting values is not a solution. At the same time, it is neither feasible nor worth trying to recreate the India of your childhood. Do not feel guilty: the U.S. model is not perfect. Be free to consciously design a composite culture synthesizing the best of the East and West. But make sure it allows individuality in choices in regard to music, food, sports, etc. Television, video games, texting, and use of a phone should be balanced and limits set to allow other priorities to take place such as chores, helping parents or siblings, homework, exercising/yoga, learning and hobbies.

- Boredom is a common and pervasive complaint of youth. Do not feel that you have to go out of your way to provide your child sensory stimulation or allow prolonged TV or video games. First accept that boredom can be attention deficit disorder, depression, loneliness, or addiction. It is the child's responsibility to accept it, tolerate it, convey his or her needs, and finally find acceptable alternatives to address it. The strength of Indian culture is introspection, sublimation, and having an inner sanctuary. Nowhere is it said that all the five senses have to be in perpetual stimulation 24/7.

Indians in Crisis

"When written in Chinese, the word "crisis" is composed of two characters – one represents danger, and the other represents opportunity."

Crisis is not unique to Indians. For example, Jews have felt it, lived through it and still today face the aftermath and the ongoing challenges to their ethnicity. We all remember the killing fields of Cambodia, the massacre in Rwanda and the genocide of the Native Americans in the USA, Maoris in Australia, and many other crises. Indians have had historical eras of prosperity but faced crisis when India was ruled/ colonized and when emigrated as indentured labors for the British, only to be betrayed when not provided with the return fare that was part of their contract. They faced multiple challenges and threats in their adopted countries, but managed to survive. Later immigrants to the West and other countries were more fortunate but the challenges to personal mental health, parenting, marriage, and family integrity have replaced the financial and survival crisis. Diaspora Indians in non-Western or non-developed countries and islands continue to suffer from political, social, and financial threats.

Indian Diaspora individuals–whether in Fiji, Suriname, Ghana, Kenya, or in the UK, Canada, or U.S–metaphorically are "Indians out of India without India being out of them." They may become flexible enough to consume alcohol socially, eat meat, and attempt to adapt to the mainstream, but deep down inside they remain grounded in Indian values. This means that family defines them as individuals and that they are required to conform to family expectations at almost any cost. Other ingrained values include the expectation of loyalty to the family hierarchy, seeing the goal of Moksha (freedom from it all), seeing attachment as the source of suffering, and practicing religion quietly, privately, without loud displays or proselytizing others.

Indian roles and responsibilities are defined hierarchically. The older generation and their dependencies are respected unconditionally, and their advice/wisdom is sought after. Children are expected to build character, play, pursue education, and respect family tradition. The middle generation is supposed to provide for all the extended family, enhance respect for the family and the name of their forefathers, empower the family to face any crisis, and meet all the challenges imposed by social and financial obligations.

Dhruv was the son of the first Queen Suniti. King Uttanapada's second wife Suruchi also had a son, and she was determined to see that her own son became the next King, rather than Dhruv. Dhruv, being the older son, was entitled to be the King. Suruchi exiled Dhruv and his mother to the forest, away from the royal palace. When Dhruv asked his mother who his father was, the queen replied that he was the Great King Uttanapada. Dhruv left the house feeling hurt and went into the forest to meditate. There were Seven Sages, who were also meditating nearby. They meditated together, and soon God Vishnu noticed the strength of Dhruv's meditation and asked what he desired. Dhruv smiled silently. God Vishnu then turned Dhruv into "The Pole Star", surrounded by bright stars around the little Dhruv-Star.

This system has worked rather successfully for Indians for the past 10,000 plus years, and has sustained Hindu civilization and minimized family disintegration in the face of the tumultuous national history of foreign aggression. It has not only kept the Diaspora connected with Mother India but also fended Indians from mental disorders, addictions, perversions, and crime. The Ashram system (described in a later chapter), the Hindu age-based social system which defines the four stages of life, has proved itself to be one of the best known mental hygiene prescriptions for allowing Indians to understand the purpose, priorities, and goals in life.

The Indian social system was relatively intact until the Islamist takeover by Babur on Feb 14th, 1483 when, under the mortal external threat, it retracted, hibernated, and isolated itself. The influence of the British Raj (1600-1947) further damaged the Indian psyche, collective pride, and the family's ability to function as an open and independent institution. In more recent times, the following factors have created a different sort of crisis, i.e. a mental health crisis:

- Increased social, financial, and emotional complexity because of recent globalization, commercialization, and consumerism.
- In the U.S., increased amounts of Indian wealth have resulted in parallel expansions in Western-style consumption. This has negatively altered the centrality of the family and its integration within the community.
- Emigration and cross-cultural exposure and the need to assimilate or adapt has thrown Indians into confusion and stress that they are not equipped to handle due to lack of experience and background.
- The trend is that the younger generation is eager to sever the "umbilical cord" at an earlier age. This results in separating, individuating, and engaging in "trial and error" behaviors, searching for autonomy and adulthood.

Indian traditions used to serve a useful mental health maintenance role but are now being let go. For example, the customary visit of all wives to their parents' house in the rainy season (saawan) allowed an acceptable regression to the girl role and distance from the stress of being a wife. It also promoted sharing and catharsis with the childhood peer group.

> *"Freud refers to 'desexualized' energy with reference to sublimation, in which case the drive is hindered from forming sexual object cathexes that might be dangerous (with a parent, for instance), and is reoriented to a non-sexual goal. Accordingly, desexualized energy will eventually discharge itself as writing, religious worship, art, or music, among other cultural, intellectual, or even sporting, pursuits."*
>
> Freud's Concept of the Death Drive and its Relation to the Superego

Similarly, events which have therapeutic value, such as Bhaiya Dauj (Brother's Day) and Holi, the spring religious festival, are losing their appeal.

The best and the most unique aspect of Indian culture was its understanding and deep grounding in the culture of sublimation. A Hindu child early on knew that there is no room for sexuality, alcohol, drugs, or wasteful leisure time. One was supposed to direct all his or her energy towards character building, rising above the mundane, and accomplishing extraordinary feats through creativity, spirituality, religiosity, or learning.

Now that it is all changing fast, Indians are stuck in a time warp and face new and unfamiliar challenges. As a consequence, Indians are showing their distress through depression, OCD, academic failures, suicide-homicide, psychosis, PTSD, anxiety disorders, manic-depression, personality disorders, and increasingly acting out through criminal behaviors. Alcohol and drug addictions are also emerging as threats. The Diaspora is not equipped and lacks any networking or resources to survive the threat to mental health that affects marriage, family, parenting and care for the older generation. It is undergoing a crisis unparalleled to any other time in the history of Indian civilization.

APATHY AS THE ROOT OF CRISIS

By some measures, it appears as though Indians and Diaspora communities are doing quite well. India boasts one of the world's fastest growing economies. In just under two decades, it has become a global force in computer software, business process outsourcing, research and development, and high-tech manufacturing. Indians in the United States are the wealthiest among all of the Diaspora countries and have the highest high school and college graduation rates of all ethnic groups, including Caucasians. They also are the country's wealthiest ethnic group, with a disproportionately large number of engineers, IT workers, and physicians, and have occupied top leadership posts in some of the country's major technological giants, including IBM, Hewlett-Packard, and Citibank.

However, in other measures, the Indian family is in crisis. Mother India is rife with poverty, illiteracy, and inadequate public healthcare. It is home to a third of the world's poor, has the largest illiterate population, and has a malnutrition rate of its youngest citizens that is twice the rate of countries in sub-Saharan Africa.

In the non-Western Diaspora, many of its citizens are victims of discrimination, terror, murder, sexual violence, forced conversions, and ethnic cleansing. As documented in the previously cited 2011 HAF Report, fundamentalists in some countries collaborate with politicians to discriminate against their Indian Diaspora citizens.

On a psychological level, the major causes of this crisis are the malaise of Hindu apathy and a collective feeling of inferiority towards the West. The apathy is the reason that, despite undeniable successes, Indians lack any systematic approach to addressing mental health needs, preventing social pathologies, and collectively addressing issues that affect the community. The sense of inferiority can be seen in the pervasive denial and disavowal of their heritage despite the widespread re-appropriation and mass-marketing of Hindu-influenced practices such as yoga, meditation, and fasting.

A prevalent stereotype is that Hindus are submissive, acquiescent, consenting, passive with an unhealthy tendency to tolerate abuse and intimidation. This negative image portrays Indians as easy targets for exploitation, manipulation, and victimization by interest groups ranging from corporations to proselytizers. The irony is that Hindus do not see the ground realities, changing demography nor the challenges to Hindu identity that threaten their existence.

An Indian wakes up praying for the well-being of the entire creation, practices non-injury, believes that all religions are as good as his own, and defines the entire world as one big family. As a result, Indians values inherent in their vocabulary and concepts, leave them ill equipped to confront adversity and process reality pragmatically. Their apathy has thus become a means for them to hide in their own imaginary cocoon and mask depression, anxiety, and fear. What's masked is neither owned nor decisively acted upon.

The Indian concept of ego is a double-edged sword. On the one hand, because of the belief that ego is the cause of all suffering, Indian projects apathy, indifference, detachment, and self-deprecation. The purpose of life is seen as Moksha, which requires systematic depletion and eventual destruction of the ego; letting go of the ego is seen as a prerequisite for good mental health as it inoculates one from narcissism, personalization, and doom and gloom. On the other hand, this concept, if taken to the extreme, risks self-degradation. What is needed is a balanced perspective that acknowledges the need for a productive executive ego applicable to changing contexts in life. West is a good role model of it.

The evolution of the Indian personality and national character has rarely been examined in the context of the collective Hindu experience through the history. The traditional Indian mental hygiene solutions, which were once easily available and culturally pervasive, are now lost, defunct or have no appeal. The breakdown of the social-family-community network has been in the making since the Muslims and British invasions. The extended family has been under assault, and it is also losing its traditional role as insurance against all odds and circumstances. If this is not reversed, then Indian society will change into an unrecognizable entity.

Western approaches to mental health diagnosis and treatment are not relevant in their entirety, or easily applicable to Indian populations due to the contextual, core personality and conceptual differences. Indians tend not to utilize formal mental health services such as psychotherapy, group sessions, and outpatient programs. Their rationalization, denial, sublimation, and attempting to cope by suffering in silence is a deterrent to becoming a consumer of mental health.

This trend continues despite the fact that Western mental health practices have made remarkable progress and contributions to human happiness. The U.S., in particular, has been the leader in applying the principles of psychology to the needs of the masses. For Indians, an ideal solution will be to blend the best of Hindu psychology and Western psychology.

Interlude: The Dreaded "H" Word

Being defensive invites negative reactions and stereotypes. To convey embarrassment, hesitation, or ambivalence about one's ethnic and religious identity is indicative of pathology i.e. neurosis of fear, trauma and a need to be accepted at any cost. Other than Hindus, no religious group shies away from owning their faith. Hindus hiding behind muteness, evasiveness, under the pretense of secularism, humbleness or spirituality is self-incriminating, encouraging others not to take them seriously and leaving their children in the lurch. Disowning one's religious/ ethnic identity is further-more indicative of low self-esteem, traumatized back-ground, and a neurotic way of coping by trying to be invisible. Such confusion is bound to result in negative stereotypes of being seen as weak, meek, complacent, pitiful and pathetic. To deny one's heritage is to be like a termite, busy destroying one's own house. To not assertively interact, participate, exchange, and negotiate with people of other religions, cultures, ethnicity, and nationalities is the ultimate act of apathy. We are social beings, and there is really no escape from being a responsible world citizen.

> "I have never found one amongst them, [the orientalists] who could deny that a single shelf of a good European library was worth the whole native literature of India and Arabia. It is, I believe, no exaggeration to say that all of the historical information which has been collected from all of the books written in the Sanskrit language is less valuable than what may be found in the paltriest abridge-ment used at proprietary schools in England."
>
> *Minute* by Lord Macaulay on the 2nd of February 1835

Some years ago I went to a cultural charity show in California organized by the local Hindu community. After the main event, there was a dinner and a collection of stalls for various organizations to showcase their work, raise funds, and attract new members. One stall, in particular, caught my attention. It had a group of three people dressed up in white gowns and tilaks on their foreheads which gave them the look of holy people who might have just walked out of a mandir on the banks of the Ganga.

More surprising to me was that two of the people were actually white Americans and so to me looked even more out of place at this gathering. The third was an American-born Indian man, and it was with him that I struck up a conversation. He explained to me that his organization was a worldwide organization that had worked for many years to teach yoga and meditation to help people lead a stress-free and peaceful life. The organization taught for free to anyone wanting to learn.

The conversation moved on, and I asked what other parts of Hinduism interested him and were taught by his group. Before I finished my sentence, he looked at me as if I had insulted his mother. "We do not teach Hinduism; we are universal," he said to me. "We do not restrict ourselves to Hinduism."

I'm not an argumentative person, but I couldn't resist pointing out that he was at an event organized by the Hindu community, that virtually everyone approaching his stall was either a Hindu or interested in Hinduism, that he was dressed in traditional Hindu dress, sacred markings on his skin, that his group had a Hindu-sounding name and that what he was offering to teach was an ancient Hindu practice and art whose ultimate aim is help the individual on the path to union with God. But this just made him angry (so much for the anger control

Spirituality is the most confused and mistakenly defined as synonymous to religion. Religions (excluding Dharma) by nature are exclusionary, monopolistic, and divisive. Guilt, and indirect threats (hell, fire, and pain) are merely a religious authority's way to control individuals and their resources. By contrast, spirituality promotes absolute secularism, total identification with the entire creation from the insignificant to the magnificent. Spirituality nurtures individuality, autonomy, transparency, democracy, and unconditional nurturing from the tiniest particle of sand to mother Earth, oceans, and the cosmos. Spirituality is anathema to religion. An individual or a professional, devoid of spirituality, simply means failure of separation and individuation process.

that his universal spiritual practice should have given him) and he insisted that all I was doing was restricting yoga by "labeling" it

Hindu. Since then I have met other members of the *Brahma Kumari* group in the U.K. and heard similar responses when I asked if they are teaching parts of Hinduism.

But it turns out that this way of thinking is more widespread than in just one or two groups. Most "gurus" who come to the West also tell their students that they are not teaching them anything that is "Hinduism." Another famous example of this is Swami Prabhupada, the late founder of the International Society for Krishna Consciousness (commonly known as the Hare Krishna Movement). Prabhupada said many times that he was not teaching Hinduism. This has led to a lot of confusion for many people who become Hare Krishnas because they are not always quite sure if they are Hindus or not.

Another place where the "H" word is avoided is in the commercial publishing world. Most Yoga books won't mention any Hindu connection. Many entrepreneurs sell Hinduism without crediting the source. When confronted, they concede that they are inspired by "traditional Indian" or "ancient Indian" stories, teachings, and history but avoid the term Hinduism. Buddhism is 'in' but Hinduism is 'out' even though Buddhism is 99% Hinduism.

Actually, I have met many Hindus who go out of their way to tell their non-Hindu friends, when asked more specifically about religion, "my parents are Hindus" or "I am spiritual, not really 'religious'". I'm not saying any of this is lying or false, but it does contrast with Christians, Muslims, and Sikhs, who always answer directly as to their faith when asked about their identity.

So the question is: why is the "H" word so bad? Most people who fall into the groups I have described so far tend to argue as follows: "Hindu" is a foreign word that doesn't fairly describe us. That's true: the actual word "Hindu" is non-Hindu in origin. But then so is the word "Indian," which is derived from the word "Hindu." So is avoiding using the word "Hindu" really any better?

Digging deeper, another reason a lot of Hindus or Hindu-influenced people do not acknowledge Hinduism is because the word "Hindu" itself has become a dirty word. "Hindu" has become associated with anything that (other) people see as negative, such as polytheism, idol worship, caste, poverty, extremism, weakness, and conservatism. Anything positive, such as art, yoga, conservation, tolerance, pluralism, music, dance, and spirituality, is seen as separate from "Hinduism."

In short, it is the same dynamics as Yehudi's preference for being called "Jewish" instead of a Jew, which is considered derogatory.

THE HEALTHY PERSONALITY

Before we move on to discuss Indian pathology, it is useful to understand the essence of what universally constitutes a healthy personality. Let's approach this from the extreme opposite and define the traits of an unhealthy personality:

- Prevalence of negative, self-defeating traits, i.e. self-degradation, giving up, leaving tasks incomplete, engaging in denials, procrastination, and dependency on others.
- Prevalence of negative habits and self-destructive lifestyle, i.e., laziness, addictions, fixation on material things, and needing or seeking excessive attention.
- Pattern of lacking balance and not being able to sustain homeostasis, i.e. disturbing and self-sabotaging one's sense of well-being by being over indulgent, obsessing about money, and seeking control over others.
- Extremes of desires, addictions, consumption and hoarding, i.e. operating excessively out of impulse or compulsions.
- Self-induced disease proneness to conditions such as obesity, hypertension, insomnia, depression, and psychosomatic disorders: conditions caused by knowingly avoiding sleep, eating excessively, or practicing a negative lifestyle.
- Prevalence of anxiety, worrying, phobias, depression, and other feeling-related disorders: conditions that are indicative

of being out-of-sync with one's social milieu and realistic expectations.

- Anger, hostility, anhedonia, guilt, and inability to relax: conditions which are indicative of a lack of skills in managing interpersonal transactions or coping with disappointments.
- Fear of being imperfect/not being in control: conditions that are indicative of inner feeling of being "damaged goods," inadequate, incompetent, and craving for others' validation.
- Fear of aging and death: conditions which are indicative of a fundamental ignorance as to the inevitability of life, thereby interfering with a person's enjoyment of the moment.
- Selfishness, self-centeredness, greed, and personal pleasure orientation (narcissism) are indicative of pathology and result in interpersonal dissatisfaction and impaired adjustment in relationships and at work.
- Expecting others to take on one's own responsibilities and living a life of feeling entitled.
- Unable to exercise a sense of personal control/self-discipline as well as a failure to enjoy personal freedom and solitude.
- Believing and acting in an exaggerated manner to advertise the superiority of one's lifestyle, religion, culture or nationality, thereby affirming a lack of spirituality and tolerance of diversity.
- Offering excuses for personal failures and avoiding confronting self, thereby indicating defensiveness that is liable to thwart any opportunity for personal growth.
- Individualism at the cost of community or family, thereby creating the possibility of isolation, alienation, and depression.
- Materialism to the exclusion of sharing, giving, and displaying charity.

Based on this long list, we can create a shorter one that defines the healthy personality:

- Skillfulness at integrating the self with society and the environment.
- Acting and behaving in the context of being a world citizen.

- Rising above and continually seeking out information, personal growth, and emotional wisdom.
- Having a democratic political ideology and appreciating transparency and diversity.
- Having a spiritually cognitive mindset that feels empathy, compassion, and oneness with all creation.
- Living life mindfully and taking responsibility for one's actions or karma, thereby sustaining emotional harmony, balance, and contentment, both internal and external.
- Nurturing everything that exists such as nature, children, women, and the elderly.
- Balancing taking with giving, i.e. practicing true sharing and unconditional commitment to mutual coexistence.
- Being thoroughly grounded in one's own separateness, individuality (autonomy) as a means of remaining creative, innovative, and integrated.

Psycho-Pathology in the Diaspora

Pathological deviations from normal behavior are a relatively recent phenomenon among the Indian Diaspora population. It may have always existed but did not enter into the social discussion or received media attention. The *To Catch a Predator* show on NBC had at least three Indian cases of adult, married men trying to engage minors in sex. Ethnic newspapers are replete with news of Indians engaging in white-collar crimes, suicides, murder-suicides, violent acting out, DUI as well as other crimes. My reviews of some of these news pointed towards mental illness such as bipolar disorder, addictions, and personality disorders.

As such, research is sketchy as to the epidemiology of mental illness, suicides and institutionalizations, etc. There is even a greater lack of research as to how to effectively diagnose or treat abnormal behaviors among Indians. At the same time, the toolkit (test batteries and treatment procedures) used by Western mental health professionals do not work with this population unless it is modified to meet this group's unique needs. Reliability and validation of these tests are also an issue. Even if the toolkit is modified, practitioners confront an array of cultural obstacles that can interfere with effective treatment. Obstacles include denial, avoidance, a lack of information and education, arrogance, guardedness, and pseudo-pride.

CULTURAL OBSTACLES

For Diaspora residents in poorer countries, the largest obstacles to optimal mental health are not cultural, but economic. Aside from not having access to mental health providers, they simply lack the financial means to contract with practitioners.

In richer countries, the obstacles are cultural and mostly involve the extreme stigma attached to seeking treatment for any non-physical ailment. Looking for help in describing this stigma, I reached out to Samir, an Indian friend, who has lived in the USA for 12 years. Samir described the stigma eloquently:

The term 'mental health' to Indians means either 'normal' or 'crazy.' By that definition, not seeing a mental health professional is 'normal.' Very few understand that treating mental issues is a science of behavior management. The social stigma of going to a mental health professional is very high (as high as having a sexual disease) and results in social rejection and branding.

Indians come from a strong religious and superstitious background where misery is karmic, and one must surrender to it. Emotional equanimity is, in essence, the core of Hindu mental health.

Some additional observations:

- The social stigma articulated above results in sweeping problems under the rug, i.e. denial.
- Loss of face and social humiliation continue to result in the avoidance of seeking help, sometimes with devastating consequences.
- Immigrant Indians display a sort of competitiveness which negatively impacts them when it comes to dealing with marital, intergenerational, addiction, and mental health issues.
- Indians often believe that their unique cultural, religious, and national background makes them immune to human weaknesses and emotional disorders. This causes a great deal of avoidance, noncompliance, and self-sabotage.
- Indians are often averse to having to pay for mental health services.
- When Indians get in trouble, they often attempt to seek out all sorts of shortcuts to get out of trouble. Thus they do not take advantage of the crisis to confront the deeper issue.
- Hindus view feelings as things to be suppressed, repressed, and brought under the control. This leaves them vulnerable to eventually acting out and losing control of repressed feelings.

- A result of the social and family structure, defined roles, and the pecking order described earlier, it is next to impossible for junior members to confront older family members. Similarly, wives do not feel that they have legitimate authority to confront those above them in the hierarchy, further curtailing healthy behavior.
- Talking is not the normal Indian mode of communicating, making it harder for mental professionals to gather data, process the information, or effectively intervene.
- Silence, depression, and turning anger and fear inward come easily to Indians due to cultural practices and values. Silently suffering is second nature to Indians. Hindus view suffering as a result of karmic factors which one has no control of, and conclude, "Why bother?"

Indians often fall victim to political exploitation, intimidation at work, and relationship conflicts or tension with neighbors. They often view illness or injury as caused by what "karmically" happens to the body, as opposed to something that is within their control. It is ingrained in the collective unconscious of Hindus that as long as one has a body, suffering is inevitable, and acceptance, surrender, and silence are the proper responses.

- Self-blame is habitually utilized either in the name of bad karma, not having done good deeds to earn right karma, or having failed in some other way. This renders impotent those who are in a position to help, confront or stop enabling the self-blame.
- Indians are phobic of separation and boundaries and, therefore continue to merge boundaries and pay a heavy price in terms of loss of freedom, autonomy, and assertion of individuality. Joint and extended families are manifestations of this tradition to keep the family together and discourage any individuation. The phenomenon continues even after immigration at a very high cost of depression, conflicts, and interpersonal damage.

- Self-sacrifice is at the core of Hindu family order. In spite of its being an overrated response, it often drives interpersonal behavior.
- Contradictions, paradoxes, and hypocrisies are accepted as part of the "big picture" of things that do not need to be resolved.

In essence, the psycho-dynamics of the Indian individual is closely tied to the family and community at large. The complexity interferes with objectivity when looking at the problem to find efficient, immediate, and direct solutions. Indirectly, it delays the diagnosis, retards getting help in time and results in difficult-to-manage, multi-layered co-morbid issues.

SUICIDE

In India, some 100,000 people per year commit suicide, at rates that have been steadily increasing for the past two decades. Although there are no comprehensive statistics, indications are that suicide rates or attempted suicide rates are also increasing in Diasporic countries, particularly the UAE, Britain, Trinidad, Malaysia, and Fiji.

- In the last two decades, the suicide rate in India has increased from 7.9 to 10.3 per 100,000.
- Studies of women in the South Asian Diaspora suggest that married women in immigrant communities are more vulnerable and at risk for suicide than native women. These studies reveal a strong link between marital, family and a wide range of health problems among Indians overseas.
- According to a 1996 study conducted by S.P. Patel and A.C. Gaw of the Department of Psychiatry, Boston University Medical Center Hospital, "suicide rates of young women immigrants from the Indian subcontinent are consistently higher than those of their male counterparts and of young

women in the indigenous populations of the countries to which they immigrate."

- Patel and Gaw (1996) found that family conflict appeared to be the precipitating factor in many suicides and that mental illness was rarely cited as the cause.
- A Malaysian study by S. Ong and Y.K. Leng reported that among residents of Kuala Lumpur, Indians form 10% of the population but account for 30% of suicides and 48% of attempted suicides.
- Although there are no comprehensive statistics, numerous reports have indicated high rates of suicides of Indian expatriates in Gulf countries. In Oman, official 2012 data indicated that one Indian commits suicide every six days, reportedly because of financial distress or personal issues. K. V. Shamsudheen, Chairman of the Pravasi Bandhu Welfare Trust in the UAE, said that high rates of suicides among unskilled and semi-skilled NRIs in the Gulf are often prompted by a financial crisis resulting from the vast gap between soaring expectation and ground reality.
- Suicide has been ranked as the leading cause of death among South Asians ages 15–24 in the United States
- Death and suicidal ideation rates for the elderly Asian-American group (which includes Indian Americans) seeking primary care are higher than for any other racial group.

General risk factors for suicide in any population are found in its psychiatric history and present symptoms (depression, schizophrenia, and alcohol dependency), social factors of isolation, unemployment, and history of past suicide attempts. Risk indicators for suicide include recent attempts, precautions taken to avoid discovery, prior communication of suicidal intent, and the completion of final acts in anticipation of death.

Among Indians in India, psychosocial stressors leading to suicide include difficulties in cultural assimilation, inter-generational conflicts, interracial and interreligious marriages, divorce, gender role conflicts, and the younger generation feeling misunderstood and unsupported by parents. Among Diaspora Indians, the immigration factor complicates the picture and challenges Indians' coping mechanisms since extended families are absent, support systems are limited, and traditional values and solutions are less available.

Some general thoughts:

- Bipolar disorder, manic depressive illness, and mood disorder play an important role in triggering suicidal behavior. As there may be a genetic component to these disorders, it is vital to know the family history and reasonable to suspect that the condition may have been passed down from generation to generation.

- It is important to watch out for adolescent behavioral changes. If adolescents suddenly act different, see if stressors such as drug abuse or depression are the cause. As children are not always comfortable talking directly to their parents, one may need to communicate subtly or involve a third party that has established a rapport with the child.

- Adult Indians living abroad in Western countries tend to be in high-stress jobs, work long hours, and lack the cultural skills to be sensitive to adolescent feelings. They are more likely to miss the clues. Moreover, Indians operate based on unspoken expectations and have difficulty coping when these are not met. Their expectations can cause severe stress, anger, and

Suicide is very threatening, disruptive and a very final act and yet it has existed in every society, religion, and culture since the beginning of the times. It is not about to disappear. Therefore society and particularly mental health professionals have a major obligation to detect it and help the person thru the process of overcoming their internal suffering, external threats and above all reallocate the purpose and direction in life. Therapeutic institutions can offer "sanctuary" until the person regains his/her composure. Police have a primary obligation to abstain from further traumatizing or criminalizing the person or the family. Suicide is always a clinical matter unless one is in such a chronic, severe, intractable, hopeless pain secondary to disease like incurable cancer. An elderly person who feels that they have lost all dignity, autonomy, and self-respect and chose not to waste their money on the health systems' heroic efforts to keep them alive should also be respected and allowed medically managed inexpensive suicide.

depression, which can turn into suicidal behavior.

- Indian family life typically revolves around work and learning, professional success, and academic performance. Parents are hyper-focused on their own high achievement and their children obtaining good grades. Stresses inherent in this focus can build up, and families may minimize the importance of stress as something that needs to be addressed.

ALCOHOLISM AND OTHER ADDICTIONS

Yes, Indians have alcohol and addiction problems.

Pramod Patel was a 34-year-old married, Gujarat born, college- educated, father of two children, who came to the USA in 1995. He had a significant head trauma caused by an auto accident and had been hospitalized for duodenal ulcers. He came for counseling because he had lost his job due to drinking. When I saw him, he was undergoing alcohol withdrawal. He had a total of three Driving While under the Influence (DUI/DWI) charges. In spite of legal requirements, he had never complied due to denials.

Diagnostically he suffered from alcohol dependence (alcoholism) and alcohol-related disorders. Since he was still in denial, no treatment was possible. His family was also not available to participate in treatment, which is a necessity. When someone has a problem with addiction, it is not uncommon that family members or significant others tend to be enablers.

It is not only the Indian community in the United States that is experiencing the growth of alcoholism. Addictions of all sorts have become pervasive throughout the world. The addiction epidemic has crossed caste, ethnic, socio-economic, and cultural barriers. Even where the use of alcohol used to be taboo, such as in Pakistan and among the upper castes of India, alcoholism has become pervasive and even accepted.

Usually thought of as a teetotaler country, India has seen a rise in alcoholism. According to the Indian Alcohol Policy Alliance, per capita consumption of alcohol increased by 106.7% over the 15-year period from 1970 to 1996. Although alcohol use is low by world standards, 80% of alcohol consumption is in the form of hard liquor. According to the January 2009 issue of *The Lancet*, the pattern of alcohol consumption in India is frequent and heavy drinking.

A growing trend in India is to view alcohol as a symbol of being modern and a requirement for "having a good time." Drinking and driving is "macho," and any suggestion that this is a dangerous behavior is laughed at. Drinking alcohol is rationalized as being "forward" or "modern," a sign of separating oneself from the "common" or "traditional" masses, who are viewed as unsophisticated.

Indians abroad tend to be more vulnerable due to their not having developed social networks, healthy routines, and recreational options. The new waves of single Indian immigrants are from villages, barely educated and working long hours for less than minimum wages. They may live in a small group that after work cooks and shares an Indian meal and enjoys it with whiskey. They may have grown up fantasizing about the day they'd have easy access to alcohol, could afford it, and could obtain it easily. They have not learned the dangers of daily drinking and have no concept of addiction. They have no awareness that there is a bigger world out there and that they have many options for socializing. They feel safe in their familiar space with their compatriots.

The newcomers lack the necessary social skills for joining the mainstream. The Indian community in their adopted land offers no orientation on how to adjust in the larger community or how to be a responsible alcohol user. They never get to deal with the emotional-cultural baggage they may have brought from home and unconsciously take refuge in long, hard evening drinking.

The degree to which Indians accept the use of alcohol seems to correlate with socio-economic class structure, caste order, exposure to Westernized educational institutions, and the type of family from which one comes.

Contributing factors include:

- Economic prosperity.
- Western influence via movies and the entertainment culture, and relaxed attitudes about alcohol use in general.
- Reduced influence of the extended family and accountability to the community.
- A switch in emphasis on learning from role models to the Western style of learning by trial and error, i.e., early autonomy and generational separations.
- Consumption orientation, i.e., instant gratification.
- Loss of culture-specific uniqueness through globalization of information and values, which includes intensified proselytization of indigenous people by non-indigenous Christian missionaries who confuse culture and nationality with spirituality.

Since addictions impact health, family, work productivity, conformation to the law, and public safety; the direct and indirect costs of addiction are beyond calculation. The fascination with alcohol and its ever increasing consumption continues in both developed and developing societies despite efforts to educate the public, modify laws, and curb marketing.

Although road fatalities and other alcohol-related impairments are increasing to the point of becoming a national epidemic, India and other developing nations have no systematic diagnostic and treatment programs for alcoholics and lack laws to handle the consequent behavior of problem drinking.

In developed countries, the severity of the problem of alcoholism and other diseases of addiction and their destructive nature has been recognized. These societies are trying to find effective ways to control and treat these diseases and contain the destruction caused by them. In the United States, voluntary organizations such as Alcoholics Anonymous (AA), Narcotics Anonymous (NA), Al-Anon (families and friends of alcoholics), Mothers Against Drunk Driving (MADD), and Students Against Drunk Driving (SADD) are multiplying to support the recovery of those who are ready to overcome their addictions. Medical and mental health professionals have accepted the challenge and are working hard to offer prevention, diagnosis, and treatment

THE OLDEST TRANQUILIZER

Gyan was 60, had an 11th-grade education, was married, and had three adult sons. His middle son suffered from Attention Deficit Hyperactivity Disorder.

Gyan originally came from an extremely deprived background and immigrated to the U.S. in 1975 with the help of a Christian missionary. His wife's family also traveled from India to live with him. Gyan worked hard and did quite well financially; eventually he retired with good health and pension benefits.

However, he suffered from severe diabetes, high cholesterol, insomnia and blindness in one eye. He had been an alcoholic for over 30 years. He was under the care of a psychiatrist and other specialists, and was taking a variety of medications for his health complications.

He preferred drinking rum, usually four shots a day alone at home. He obsessively complained that his wife sided with her mother and her brother. This made him very angry as he felt abandoned. He had chronic marital problems, and his wife eventually gave up on him. He came to seek help only because his wife threatened to put him in jail, and he felt scared. His wife wanted to separate from him, but he didn't want to. His life revolved around his wife, children, home, and money-making, and he had no other life and was ill prepared for changes in his life.

Diagnostically, he suffered from alcoholism, marital problems, and parent-child problems. Psycho-dynamically, in spite of his denials, rationalizations, and pattern of blaming others, his problems revolved around alcoholism. He grew up as an orphan and seemed destined to end up as an orphan, all alone. His wife and children lost all respect for him. The harder he tried to cling to the family, the more alienated he felt. He was not open to psychological or alcohol treatment and thus kept relapsing. The last I heard, his depression had worsened, he had become totally blind and was divorced.

A HINDU VIEW OF ADDICTIONS

Hindus do not view addiction as a disease but as a character defect. This desire is viewed as the core of all pathology. Giving in to desire and acting on desire "fuel the fire." Desire is the core of all human suffering, operating through human senses. Most of the early psychologists have affirmed the role of the senses in pathology; however, the concept of desire is originally Hindu. Western psychology only now is recognizing the role of desire in human pathology and suffering.

Society can hold on to the ideals of male-female virginity. However, the desires and, in particular, sexual urges often drive human behavior. Mere religion, moral ideals, or even sublimation cannot prevent sexual acting out, desires, or preoccupation. Denials or evasiveness only further complicate the relationships between genders. The best options are to own human sexuality as a powerful reality, promote sublimation, provide education and skills to meet sexual needs appropriately and yet hold on to the social ideals as they work like a prophylactic and promote exceptional growth. Deviancy, psychopathy, perversions, and sexual violence like rape should be treated like any other crime.

Addictions come in a cluster or as a syndrome and never alone. This is because desire inevitably needs and uses the five senses, and, notably, all the orifices of the body. Following the Western model, it is no longer enough to simply and separately enjoy the pleasures of eating, drinking, entertainment, and sexual relations. The psycho-dynamics of alcoholism, drug and food addictions, object and attachment obsessions, and sexually deviant behaviors can be explained effectively in the desire model of emotional drive.

Happiness is a state of mind in which one is content and free from the perpetual pull of the senses and the push of desire. In the traditional Hindu view, the goal of life is not to pursue pleasure (serving the senses), but to become totally free from the bondage of pleasure and pain. For consumption-oriented, free-market Western economics to survive, addictions are essential.

The individual response to this materialistic imperative is depression, withdrawal, and aggression, acting out, phobias, perversions, panic attacks, obsessive-compulsive disorder, and character disorders. Pleasure and pain are tied together in addiction: pleasure leads to addiction, and that leads to pain.

TREATMENT OPTIONS FOR NON-WESTERN ALCOHOLICS

Currently, the most effective approach to the treatment of alcoholism is found in the wisdom of Alcoholics Anonymous (AA), a program based on action and spiritually. If the techniques of Hindu psychology are added to the principles of AA, the combined approach not only would treat addictions successfully, it could be used to create happiness and even Nirvana.

Although Alcoholics Anonymous offers the best hope for the treatment and rehabilitation of alcoholics, its success rate ranges between 30 and 40 percent. Western psychology and medicine have proven to be of little value in the rehabilitation of alcoholics, leaving 60 to 70 percent of alcoholics without any hope. Non-Western and many Western addicts resist AA. They and their families suffer in utter helplessness. With the majority of active alcoholics not being treated effectively, exploring and applying other approaches and cross-cultural methods are of critical importance.

Therapy should focus on the following:
- Helping the patient become more sensitive and aware of objective reality, confronting him with facts, statistics, and second opinions.
- Strengthening the patient's capacity to confront his weaknesses and deficiencies.
- Helping the patient identify and productively use his or her gifts and strengths.
- Helping the patient develop less pretentious and illusory

attitudes and behaviors.

- Helping the patient develop realistic and spiritually-based insights and behaviors.
- Treating the comorbid pathology of addiction. For example, depression in many cases is the comorbid condition behind the addiction. For Indians, it may be difficult to perceive depression as many do not allow themselves to "feel feelings." In this case, alcohol use masks the underlying depression.

Therapeutic methods that can be employed include:
- *Letter-writing.* Talking does not happen easily. Moreover, some people are not that creative. I think it is much more effective if the significant others were to write letters to the addict. Letters should be honest, thoughtful, and direct and can even be confrontational. It gives everybody room to save face, convey their exact feelings and concerns, and above all, it gives everyone concerned time to process.
- *Environmental management.* Change the association of "people, places, and things" to environments where alcohol or drug consumption is absent.
- *Psychopharmacological intervention.* Medications such as Antabuse, Dolophin, Revex, Narcan, and Buprenex can help manage the condition.
- *Behavior modification.* There are a number of techniques aimed at teaching the patient to transform self-destructive behaviors into productive, health-generating ones.
- *Cognitive reorientation and introspection.* The goal is to help patients recognize, interrupt, and redirect their addiction compulsions.
- *Family therapy.* To promote a realistic view of self and and to learn the interpersonal skills of frankness and assertiveness without fearing disapproval and shame.
- *Identifying passive-aggressive or dependent personality disorders.* These require longer-term treatment.
- *Offering orientation courses.* These can be offered to Diaspora

newcomers in Hindu temples (Mandirs). The orientation's goal should be to promote healthy acculturation and address socialization skills.

- *Re-create healthy homeland imitations (Little Indias).* Immigrants are likely to do this in some form, but can be encouraged to strengthen these inward havens as a means of sustaining their Indian identity without the risk of alcoholism, drug dependence, or acting out. They can re-create their homelands through simple practices such as speaking their language, listening to familiar music, and cooking native meals.

TWELVE-STEP ALTERNATIVE

Without a doubt, the most effective treatment method for people struggling with various forms of addiction is a AA recovery group that employs a Twelve-Step Program.

The major concerns that some have with these programs is that it is based on Christianity/religion. Many view AA and recovery movements as unscientific. Some prefer cognitive behavioral means rather than join "drunks" repeating their stories of drunken days. In my clinical practice of the past 45 years, I have had many individuals who were unable to relate to or participate in AA model.

Spirituality and religion are different; first is above any thinking of being in or out or labeling any one is infidel or "not saved". Following is an outline of an alternative 12 step program.

1. We acknowledge our being a microcosm in a large universe, and therefore, ego must be stripped away.
2. We acknowledge that desire is the source of all suffering, and therefore, must be surrendered to spirituality.
3. We acknowledge the need to surrender our arrogance and accept outside resources and help.
4. We take full responsibility for all of our actions and

consequences.

5. We acknowledge the need for ongoing growth and integration by overcoming our character defects.

6. We acknowledge the need to live meditatively and refrain from excessive consumption.

7. We commit to self-help through being in the company of others who are in recovery.

8. We will make recompense to all those that we have hurt, offended, exploited and neglected.

9. We will commit to a lifestyle of non-injury to anyone or anything.

10. We will accept mentoring by an experienced recovering person, qualified professional or a wise adult.

11. We will live in the moment, and avoid living in the past or in the imagined future.

12. We will refrain from illusions, clinging to things, acting out of likes and dislikes, and narcissism.

THE INDIAN PSYCHOPATH

The Diagnostic and Statistical Manual of Mental Disorders IV (DSM) describes psychopaths, sociopaths, and those with antisocial personalities as people who lack all empathy with others. They do not abide by the social, religious, or legal norms and are utterly self-centered. These individuals may use people, lie, have a sporadic job history, have a criminal record, and can inflict violence on others.

However, due to cultural variables, Indian psychopaths do not necessarily have criminal records, have a pattern of drug or alcohol abuse, and engage in promiscuity, practice violence, or break religious or social rules. They are harder to detect because their culture allows typical disguises. Psychopathy comes to play in relationships, friendships, or when one encounters individuals during transitions, such as traveling, on pilgrimages, etc. A typical transaction will start with the psychopath asking a small favor but then escalating the request into a full-fledged one, such as borrowing a large sum of money or expecting to be sponsored to come abroad. Sometimes, the initial contact will be a plea for help like needing money for school, college, or to pay off a loan. But then the game will exacerbate, and the request will be repeated again and again. The irony is that it all takes place without any shame, gratitude, or consideration for the helper's feelings. If the helper acquiesces, it will usually end with the helper losing money, relationships, and all further communication.

These individuals tend to hide behind various professional or cultural disguises. They may have religious titles such as *panda* (Hindu scholar), *pujari* (Hindu priest), *maulwi* (Muslim religious scholar) or *imam* (Muslim priest). They may also hide behind professional roles and layers of bureaucracy and be clerks, police, government employees, politicians, physicians, and jurists.

The following describes the characteristics of the Indian psychopath.

- Charming, overly polite, down-to-earth, exaggerated modesty in outward behavior.
- Language is carefully chosen to come across as honest, trustworthy, simple, and without any agendas or ulterior motives.
- The tone and quality of voice are the master clue. Psychopaths will ensure that their voice is tender, soft, gentle, polite, non-assertive, and almost boyish and feminine during communication. This tone is used to prepare the ground for a follow-up surprise or demand for a favor. It's a remarkable tool utilized most efficiently to disarm you so that you cannot dare say no.
- Physical appearance is highly conventional, religious or prim and proper and calculated to create an image of being authentic, genuine, and reassuring.

- Underneath this facade, the Indian psychopath is highly calculating, utterly selfish, and constantly maneuvering. The Indian word for maneuvering is *jugad*. The interesting aspect is that jugad and hustling, manipulating, and testing others never stops. Your space is constantly invaded, and any and all contact proves injurious to the weak.
- He never honors commitments, contracts, or agreed-upon terms and conditions.
- He privately engages in hedonistic pleasures such as drinking or gluttonous eating.
- He lacks empathy, and is driven by the promise of material gain. Uses lying, cheating, and any means to selfish end.
- He goes out of the way to appear accommodating, but underneath schemes to steal, take advantage, or set the victim up in some complex triangle to gain benefit.
- He may engage in very controlled and highly sneaky sexual exploitations while claiming to be pious, pure, or religious.

IT'S NOT ME; EVERYONE ELSE IS CRAZY

Gayatri was a 45-year-old, Chennai-born Hindu female. She had an adolescent son and a daughter, and her husband was a computer professional. She had two masters' degrees and was employed until the birth of her son. She had been married for 20 years. Her daughter was doing well in college while the son was living at home and showed severe dysfunction by being immature, angry, and underperforming in school.

Gayatri preferred to see me alone. During the session, she presented herself as "all together," in control of her life and put the blame on her daughter and husband. She was worried about her son while she described her daughter as being a slut and an alcoholic. However, other sources revealed that Gayatri has been irrational, paranoid, psychotic, and was impossible as a mother and a wife. She had many consultations but was always noncompliant with following up and medications. She'd often impulsively leave her family and go to India for long periods. She acted violent towards her husband. The court restricted her involvement with the children.

She was suffering from schizophrenia, paranoid-type with brief psychotic episodes, marital problems, and parent-child relational problems.

After the initial session, she left for India for an indefinite period. She kept in touch with me via emails worrying about her son, and whether he kept his appointments. However, her husband had an excuse that the son did not want to come for counseling.

DELUSIONAL DISORDER

DSM-IV defines delusional disorder as a non-psychotic, somewhat reality based misconception-of-self behavior that is without any significant impairment of functioning. This behavior may be accompanied by tactile or olfactory hallucinations. Types of delusional disorder are based on themes including: erotomanic, grandiose, jealous, persecutory, somatic, mixed type, or unspecified.

Anecdotally speaking, the grandiose type is the most prominent among Indians. It manifests in social situations and is accompanied by the overwhelming need to impress others.

Typically, Indians' hyperbole pertain to the following themes:
- Ayurveda is superior to all other systems of medicine.
- India is the best country in the world; its people are. This belief is rooted in the need to prove that Western/European cultures are not as good, kind, sincere, and honest as Indian culture.
- Indian civilization is the oldest and is the most evolved.

THE THOUSAND FACES OF FEAR

Abdul was a 33-year-old single, U.S. raised Muslim who lived with his parents and younger brother. His sister was married and lived on her own. His mother was a housewife, and his father a physician. When Abdul was attending medical school, he had his own apartment.

He had consulted a few psychiatrists but had not responded well to medications. He came to see me sporadically and was able to trust and comply. He was suffering a great deal but had avoided psychological counseling. His symptoms included severe impairment as to attention, concentration, focusing. He showed signs of obsessive compulsivity, phobias, fears, and social anxiety. He suffered bouts of extreme rage and irrational behavior, putting himself and the family in danger. Having had unreasonable grandiose demands from his father, he also exhibited catastrophizing and anticipated doom and gloom. He stalked his girlfriend and felt he could not survive without clinging to her.

He was suffering from Bipolar Disorder II, mixed, rapid cycling, obsessive-compulsive disorder, and parent-child conflict. His delusional disorder was the erotomanic type.

Psycho-dynamically, his fear of separation, independent living, and entrance to an adult role evoked a pervasive sense of helplessness and an anticipation of failure. His demanding, clinging, aggressive behavior towards his father was actually a cover-up for his intense fear and lack of self-confidence. He did not trust his feelings or faculties, with regard to seeing, hearing, interacting, judgment, and decision-making.

He responded well to individual and family psychotherapy and acquired skills for identifying, tolerating, and verbalizing his feelings (happiness, sadness, anger, fear, anxiety, and jealousy). His family respected his interest in yoga, and occasional alcohol use. Eventually he married and transitioned into a remarkable adulthood.

Indians and Mental Health

"The sorrow which has no vent in tears may make other organs weep."

- Henry Maudsley

As a consumer of mental healthcare, the Indian patient is minimally aware, totally uninvolved, and rarely proactive. In the words of S.A., an Indian patient, "Indian people do not take mental health professionals seriously and fear stigma and social ostracism." He felt that in most Indian families, the head of the household handles "in-house" major conflicts relating to relationships. Regardless of the source of the conflict, Indians do not trust an outsider's opinion. S.A. suggested that the Indian consumer needs to be educated on the nature of the mental health profession, the benefits of counseling, and the consequences of not seeking help.

As it inherently implies that they have failed and are weak, an Indian patient's decision to consult a mental health professional is an overwhelming experience. It also exacerbates their sense of vulnerability and loss of control. Feeling emotions and processing them is an unfamiliar concept for Indians, since they have been taught since birth to suppress, repress, or conceal them. Indians mostly *intellectualize* instead of *recognizing and owning* their feelings, whether sorrow, anger, fear, or worry. They approach life as a task, and their coping mechanism is to be robotic or mechanical.

Denial: Hindus even have a word for it called *maya*, meaning all of creation is nothing but an illusion due to its perpetually changing nature. This is the perfect example of profound denial. Everything is transient and therefore nothing is to be taken seriously but merely observed dispassionately. This mindset is not limited to spirituality but goes into dealing with suffering, emotional or otherwise. Besides lacking information about the utility of mental health services, denial is a major factor that prevents Indians from seeking help.

This denial mechanism is rather complex, as it makes Indians not see the problem, imagining it will automatically disappear. Denial involves engaging in elaborate rationalizations, simplifications, oversimplifications, or inappropriate remedial measures. Indians invented cognitive-behavioral therapy without ever calling it so. They define desire as the cause of all suffering and, therefore, confront themselves to annihilate it by seeing all objective reality as maya, or choosing detachment.

Take the case of Vineet. (who had a 10-year-old daughter from a previous marriage) His second wife felt abandoned, depressed, agitated and withdrawn. They came to get help because the school noticed that the daughter was having bruises and was suffering from malnourishment. When they came to see me, they had already decided to ship the girl to a boarding school in India. The father and the grandfather's logic was that she would get a good spiritual education in the Indian cultural context. It took only a few sessions to identify that the step-mother was redirecting her own desperation to the daughter to get back at the husband; She felt trapped in caring for her own infant and step-daughter, while not receiving any adult attention. After only a few sessions, the entire family developed a very open communication and the entire crisis ended. Follow-up marriage therapy sessions continued since the husband lacked the skill to empathize with his wife and address her emotional needs.

Shipping the children to live with grandparents or family members in India and schooling there is a common practice among Gujarati immigrants. It does not take into consideration the child's feelings, emotional needs and attachments to parents and peers.

Social Situations: Indians have serious difficulty in curtailing and altering their private behavior while in social situations. They see the social aspect as an extension of the personal space and private world, which causes them to pay a heavy price.

Cultural crossfire: Indians in India do not face the same

confusion, self-doubts, or obsess with the issue of "Who am I?" These issues become very prominent and emotionally draining for Indians who are living abroad and have to interact with other cultures, values, or expectations. I recall in a social gathering an Indian jokingly saying, "My wallet is here, but my heart is in India."

Let's take the case of the young Indian man who was arrested for walking nude on the median of a highway in New Jersey. When I interviewed him, he said that he was "walking the middle of the road," meaning acting out his ambivalence about being an Indian, having to live in America, and not being able to emotionally reconcile the two.

Even though the Indian Diaspora population has rapidly increased and almost all major cities have "Little Indias" where Indian communities have become concentrated, Indians continue to feel split between India and their host countries, and between Eastern and Western values. The result sometimes manifests as emotional distress and disorders such as engaging in crimes, being ticketed for DUI, or acting out at work.

Self-insulation: Indians have a difficult time accepting feelings of vulnerability, not being in control, being exposed, or being the center of attention. They insulate themselves from feelings of inadequacy or incompetence. The cover-up can involve resorting to alcohol, an obsession with money, excessive religiosity, or more complex masking, such as intellectual pursuits, professional preoccupations, and grandiosity. It is not uncommon that Indians who self-insulate glorify India at the expense of the countries in which they live.

Externalizers: The opposite of self-insulators are the externalizers who have difficulty dealing with their feelings, coping with alienation, and being in unfamiliar situations. Such persons may engage in social drinking, visit gentleman's clubs, and might even show up on the NBC show "To Catch a Predator."

Over Protectiveness: By and large, Indian parents find it very difficult to tolerate the separation and autonomy of their children or adolescents. They use education as a tool to exercise control to protect their children from exposure to risky behaviors. Although this has its usefulness, it also adds to children's stress and finding a balance between their home culture and the outside world.

Indian parents show extreme fear of their children dating or exploring their sexuality. The parents of a fifth grader brought him to see me because of poor academic performance. When I evaluated him, it became very clear that he was suffering from a learning disability and also had ADHD. Following the feedback, the parents became non-compliant to treatment. I later learned that they had "solved" the problem by relocating to a different school district.

Masking the symptoms: Indians have difficulty dealing with mental disorders such as depression and alcoholism due to their sense of failure and being weak. They tend to be extremely self-critical but also naive as to the nature of the disease and the value of professional help. They also deal with their internal conflicts by avoiding any association or affiliation with their religion, community, and country. Their aversion tends to be highly exaggerated and extreme and may manifest by their choosing to Americanize or Christianize their names and disown anything Indian.

Obsessive compulsivity: Although Alcoholics Anonymous invented the approach of "Keeping It Simple Stupid," Indians have perfected it by limiting their focus to being driven towards professional perfection and business entrepreneurship, earning and hoarding money. This is a kind of obsessive-compulsive disorder that is an Indian trademark.

It is difficult for an Indian to tolerate being in a gray area. Even after getting married, Indians, particularly males, tend to cling obsessively to parents and siblings who might be thousands of miles away. This clinging behavior shows up via daily or weekend long-distance calls, sending money to them regularly and failing to entertain their spouses without including their extended family or friends. At the same time, husbands might micromanage their spouses and children with the aim of protecting them from any unforeseen, unimaginable crisis.

External locus of control: On the one hand, Indians like to be in control to avoid feeling vulnerable. But, on the other hand, they relinquish their sense of control by handing it over to others. Indians' need for approval, validation, acknowledgment, testimonials, and compliments by others is an ever-present phenomenon. It is not good enough for Indians to be proud of their Vedas, Indian medicine, vegetarianism or an Indian female being an astronaut, unless and until Caucasians, Westerners, or the English media acknowledges it. The Indian sense of power—being externally located—creates a paradoxically opposite stereotype of being seen as meek, weak, complacent, insecure, and people-pleasing.

CULTURAL COMPETENCE & SERVICE DELIVERY

All human beings have their own somewhat unique perceptions of themselves, others, and the world. Each culture and religion define the self somewhat differently. These perceptions drive behavior and determine the makeup of individual personalities. As stated elsewhere, belief systems, concepts, and values determine one's internal as well as external behavior.

Each culture evolves in a particular psycho-socio-econo-geo-political context. In Islam, essentially a desert culture, people eat together from the same dish while in the West each person has his or her own dishes and cutlery. Even water is not sipped from the same glass. In India, guests are welcome any time of the day and night, and without any advance notice. In Africa, a tribal chief faces in all four directions and yells out loud, "Please come and join us as we are about to start eating."

Similarly, every culture has its own vocabulary for mental illnesses and procedures to treat them. For example, in India, until recently, there was no word for anxiety, post-traumatic stress disorder, or even depression. Worrying was referred to as *chinta*, and all sadness, including pain was *dukh*. The vocabulary was simple, and so were the manifestations. Suffering was seen to be either due to karma or the consequences of prior bad karma. Unlike Freudian psychology, the logic was simple, and there was never any need to blame parents, childhood, bad experiences, or others. In other words, the pervasiveness of "acceptance and surrender" was a proactive mechanism for preventing any doom and gloom or mental breakdown.

It should be obvious that the Indian patient needing mental health services cannot be approached casually or superficially. Also, he cannot be easily educated about his role in the treatment or engagement in the therapeutic process. Due to lack of awareness about the utilization of clinical psychology, the patient, in spite of the distress, will not have the skills to benefit from, nor the willingness to, engage in a Eurocentric-oriented therapeutic culture.

However, an Indian patient does understand how to be a good patient to a medical doctor. No matter how inconvenient, he will comply rather religiously with all prescribed dietary restrictions. But when it comes to dealing with feelings, the traditional Indian patient approaches his emotional distress via sharing with the nearest available elderly, wise man, monk, pundit, or some other senior person. He is not worried about confidentiality. He is merely seeking direction, advice, words of wisdom, or reassurance that his problems are transient, and there is no reason to feel despondent. Trusting is also built in since he is seeking the advice of older, experienced and mature people. It could not be any simpler.

The same is not true when it has to do with mental health or sexual issues in the modern context. Indians traditionally have not seen mental health issues as a problem and certainly are not accustomed to reaching out for help. As a result, an Indian patient more often than not is a challenge for the mental health professional.

I remember a case of a young Indian Muslim boy who was asked by the school to seek help. After initial feedback, his family chose to change the school rather than to deal with the issues. The family could not conceive that they would be exposed to others. I know they would have even gone back to India rather than consulting mental health, marital, or family counseling in the U.S.

As mentioned earlier, it is vital to understand that Indian families and marriages exist and function around a very delicate system based on faith, duties, traditions, rituals, and hierarchies. Any probing, attempt to introduce change or encourage one to identify with their feelings can be destructive or at least debilitating. Indian families do not have contingency alternatives such as divorce, separation, or remarriage. They also lack contingency plans on how to care for children in case of divorce. This lack of contingency plan is one of the reasons that Indian spouses act out dangerously: they have never thought of how to get out of a marital trap or renegotiate a new emotional contract. It's all or nothing.

The reader must keep in mind that similar observations will not apply to the same extent to an Indian client who has been living in the West and certainly not to the one who has been born and brought up in the USA, Canada, or in the UK. This is for the simple reason that they are exposed to counselors and mental health professionals early on in the school or through media.

However, the older generation remains heavily influenced by the cultural past and historical legacies. The differences are pervasive and apply not only as to the perception of the mental health service provider, but also to how to hand over personal information, deal with feelings, or talk to an outsider about secret family matters. The older generation also feels that their distress is merely a consequence of their own deeds or karma, and has to be lived through, and not escaped. This deeply held value system of acceptance and resignation are also major barriers toward convincing the patient that change is possible, and that taking control of one's feelings, and of their life's course is an option.

Indian self-help rituals are also considered to be important adjuncts to seeking professional help. For example, fasting, religious rituals, and varieties of self-sacrifice are often utilized to cope with or stop the suffering. In addition, Indian Ayurvedic dietary practice holds that changing what one eats can cure the ills of the body-mind. Different foods are categorized in terms of their properties, and certain combinations are prohibited due to their ill effect on the body. For example, one is not supposed to drink water after eating peanuts. Similarly, one is prohibited from eating sour foods or beverages if one is coughing or has a sore throat. And fasting is practiced if one is suffering from fever. The very first step an Indian takes is to reduce or stop the consumption of salt, oil, and chilies to bring the body back to balance. In olden days and currently at the village level, certain abnormal behaviors are dealt with through purification rituals and shamanic approaches. The belief here is that the individual is under the control of some evil spirit. The "evil eye" may also be viewed as a cause of a mental disorder. The thought behind this is that life is so simple, basic, routine, and predictable that one rarely sees an episode of mental disorder. So when a disorder occurs, the etiology is seen as coming from outside the person. However, this perspective is changing rather rapidly as alcoholism, suicides, and homicides are on the rise.

In essence, Hindus tend to see emotional and even physical problems as a result of an internal imbalance or bad karma. Imbalance is interpreted in terms of either lack of self-discipline, bad habits, or external evil influences. As a result, the therapist has to be sensitive to the patient's value system and needs to examine his lifestyle, food intake, failures to be good, and defending to not see the problem in interpersonal, family, stress-related terms. Any professional treating an Indian cannot ignore these factors as part of the overall treatment.

INTERACTING WITH PATIENTS

As to therapy, the initial contact sets the pace of the progress and outcome. It is conceivable that the potential patient is not interested in consulting, nor believes that talk therapy is meaningful. She may believe there is a better use of her money and time, and may only be coming because of some external mandate, such as pressure from her employer, a court order, or a threat of divorce. She thinks that even one consultation is a waste of time, and may try to look courteous, pleasant, and even cooperative. Underneath this façade, she is eager to get out of your office as soon as possible.

As a mental health professional, you have only one chance to make it all work. First impressions matter, particularly when a patient is coming from a cultural background where it is uncommon to seek mental health help or reveal sacredly held personal and family details. One can imagine what concerns, anxiety, reservations and confused expectations the person may be bringing with him. These apprehensions often cause the patient not to keep the appointment, cancel at the last minute, or come late. Another response is to arbitrarily change the ground rules and expect to have the session on the phone. I have also seen instances in which the patient does not get the clues to end the session and instead engages in prolonging it. This is because the patient has a rapport with you but because he is paying and wants to maximize his return.

Some of these issues are better handled by first focusing on the non-clinical matters, i.e., telling the patient that you are extremely busy and successful and that without him becoming your patient, you will still be fine. In other words, you do not need his business. This may seem rather crude, but I have often used it to clear a patient's misconception that all you care about is your fee.

I also ask all my patients if they have any fee limitations and if they want to discuss needing some exceptions. I make it very clear that in the future all money transactions will be handled by the secretary, including phone contacts and scheduling appointments.

If the patient is not sophisticated enough, explain – at the outset – the office culture and routine, your value system about money, and the importance of mutual punctuality. Indian patients respond better if the professional carries out the initial pre-session contact rather than the office staff. The focus of the pre-session should be a mutual introduction, explanation of psychotherapy and how it works, what the patient can expect, and office policies regarding short-notice cancellations, fees, payment methods, etc. It will also help to mail the patient an appointment card and clear directions to avoid last minute frenzied calls that he cannot figure out how to get to the office.

Additional considerations:
- Provide a structure in which to listen, but also, clarify concepts like what it means to have professional boundaries; spell out what you will and will not do as a professional. It should be very clear that you will not discuss payment and appointment issues again. The patient must know that you do not want to be called at odd hours or contacted at home. Remind the patient that they must see office staff for scheduling appointments. Training the patient to honor boundaries is the first step to successful therapy.
- Sometimes psychological testing may be necessary, as well as referring the patient for a second opinion, either to establish a diagnosis or to manage the illness. The patient deserves to have such information explained so that they may be prepared.

The patient's expectations must be clarified to remove any confusion, discrepancies or misunderstanding. It should be conveyed that there are no shortcuts and that the entire process is carried out legitimately in accordance with professional ethics, insurance rules, and within the prescribed norms. You may encounter patients who pursue shortcuts in place of therapy. An example is a patient who once offered me a bribe to write him a letter saying that he was not an alcoholic and that he had completed his treatment for DUI.

HANDLING THE PRELIMINARIES

The need to take care of the mechanics and to remove any emotions from the process cannot be overemphasized. In my office, we negotiate this aspect three times: on the phone before the actual appointment, via a follow-up signed contract after the phone appointment, and at the beginning of the first session. Taking the time to get clarity on these issues will allow the clinical focus to go uninterrupted without any unnecessary games, such as the patient trying to renegotiate fees. If feasible, the clinician should in this first phase give the patient some idea as to approximately how many sessions will be essential. Because only short-term therapy is acceptable to many Indian clients, even the very first session should be approached as total therapy from diagnosis to feedback. In that case, the patient has all necessary information even if he does not return. I always encourage my patients to find a practitioner that is near their home or more convenient than I as to distance. I have found that the best cure for the Empire State Building-size Indian ego is to deflate it very early by conveying you are happy to help them find someone else.

OVERVIEW OF THE TREATMENT PROCESS

Each patient is unique and requires individualized treatment planning. Once the patient is educated about the process, the clinician can concentrate on diagnosis and treatment. I recommend a three-phase approach with Indian and Asian clients. In each of these phases, avoid a process-oriented approach in favor of a more directed one, using behavioral prescriptions. Teaching, modeling, and providing task assignments work much better than sharing and processing feelings. Although Indian patients' built-in obsessive-compulsiveness can seem like a barrier to growth, it is paradoxically also an asset and can be utilized to effectively engage the patient in accomplishing certain tasks. For example, the assignment of specific readings, or watching a particular movie, can be excellent tools to clarify certain concepts or teach skills.

Initial Phase: During the initial diagnostic interview and observation, help the patient conduct an inventory of her strengths and weaknesses as a means of uncovering the pattern that is tied to the problematic behavior. At the same time, highlight her character strengths and how she can utilize them to solve domestic problems, achieve success at work, speed up adjustment, or enhance security. This is not always easy, as I have had many patients who were highly educated and professionally successful but were unable to relate their feelings to their behavior or understand the concept of introspection. It is also difficult for some patients to see the impact of their behavior on others (significant or outsiders) or to have awareness as to how others feel.

Human history is a record of violence, testosterone superiority, and praises of the courageous. The likes of Buddha, Ashoka the Great, and Mahatma Gandhi highlighted the importance of non-violence. Human beings, in my view, will always resort to violence since prolonged peace can become very boring. Violence and injury are here to stay and will continue to engage human beings in a perpetual dance. The challenge for psychologists is to offer techniques to prevent, minimize, and manage wars, dictatorships, abuse, violence, exploitation, subjugation, human trafficking, child labor, suicides, etc., which result in depression, worrying, fears, panic attacks, manic depressions, addictions, psychosis, and emotional traumas. On a community and individual level, psychologists need to extend themselves to recognizing the warning signs among the youth population for harming self or others. Some problems are negative outbursts, excessively risky behavior, injuring self, others or animals, verbal threats, inappropriate attention-seeking, affiliating with bullies, gangs or substance abusers, abrupt behavior changes such as hyper-somnia, insomnia, detachment, loss of self-esteem, giving personal things away, and impaired school grades. It will require a team effort and be best accomplished by working together with teachers and parents.

For example, a software engineer I worked with after several sessions was still not fully convinced that the simple act of occasionally bringing home a red rose for his wife would make her feel special. His wife had clearly asked for this gesture, as he was routinely giving flowers to her aunt. He kept telling me that his wife was the most important person in his life and that thinking this was sufficient. In other words, he believed that his thinking was adequate and thus action was unnecessary.

Middle Phase: During this phase, highlight and educate the patient about the diagnosis, and provide written information describing it. Point out the risks and consequences if the condition is untreated, i.e., the impact of the symptoms and unresolved problems on the family, finances, and future. You can also ask the patient to do some homework and learn about their illness. Recommend specific book-reading or movie-watching tasks to facilitate understanding. I routinely demand that alcoholic patients read the "Big Book" published by Alcoholics Anonymous. With the popularity of Internet, the task of finding relevant material has become very easy.

The patient usually needs help neutralizing negative feelings (anger, fear, sadness, anxiety, worrying, guilt, shame, failure, unworthiness, split between conflicting roles and obligations, helplessness). Such distress typically is rooted in excessive, often incompatible demands of being in different roles, such as husband, parent, child, and sibling. Unlike in the Western culture, an Indian continues to feel responsible as well as obligated to carry out his expected roles without any modification, even after marriage, becoming a father, or emigrating abroad. Sometimes these responsibilities are externally imposed and obligatory, but most often they are self-imposed and help the patient feel good about herself and gain acceptance from significant others.

Often, negative feelings are connected to unmet expectations. For example, sons, daughters, or daughters-in-law may feel let down by significant others. As a result, they lose respect for those who have not met their expectations. They may feel guilt and anguish about their lack of respect, which may result in depression, rage or acting out. Until recently, Indians did not externalize these symptoms and primarily reacted to them solely on the thinking level. However, this is changing, and Indians are becoming more emotionally expressive in their reactions.

Final Phase: As the risk of abrupt termination, noncompliance or no-shows is very high, it is very important to educate the patient about the process of therapy termination. She should be assisted and encouraged to make a list of post-treatment goals. The list should be specific, simple, and relevant to her situation. If she is receptive, monthly follow-up sessions can also be scheduled. Clearly emphasize the need for follow-up, whether this involves meeting with other physicians, taking medication, lifestyle changes, or engaging in self-help solutions.

THERAPIST OPTIONS

Where do you start? How does one distinguish between types of therapists? How can you find a culturally competent therapist? What approach should you take when you are in crisis?

There are basically four types: psychiatrists, psychologists, counselors, and social workers. Psychiatrists, due to their training and medical orientation, see mental problems as disorders of brain chemistry or some physical etiology and tend to prescribe medicines. They can admit and discharge patients in and out of crisis centers and hospitals. This is slowly changing, and psychologists are starting to become affiliated with the hospitals and have admitting and discharging privileges.

Psychologists, on the other hand, tend to define emotional problems more in terms of conflict with feelings, distorted thinking, lacking behavioral, interpersonal, and decision-making skills. Their treatment orientations tend to be teaching, modeling, and promoting awareness of the patient's behavioral, cognitive, and emotional ineffectiveness patterns and confusions as well as unproductive habits. Psychologists accomplish their goals by utilizing verbal interaction, imagery, role-playing, behavioral management, modifications, and so on to alter the patient's behavior.

A professional and ethical mental health provider will know his limitations of expertise and will be able to make choices on which will be the right specialty for referral. Psychologists utilize numerous strategies to treat different conditions. A well-trained or experienced psychologist will not hesitate to refer the patient for psychiatric and neurological consultation, interacting with the primary care provider (PCP), endocrinologist, cardiologists, or other specialists to ensure that patients get the most comprehensive and effective treatment. A good psychologist like a good PCP is the first line of defense. He can act as a gatekeeper and coordinate the entire treatment process unlike a psychiatrist, who does not have enough time or is primarily limited to prescribing medicines.

Licensed Professional Counselors are trained in general psychotherapy and assisting clients with various life problems (e.g., relationships, career, and overall well-being). While licensed counselors can provide some evaluation services, they are much more limited in scope compared to psychologists.

The role of Social workers is interventions at the social level. Licensed Clinical Social Workers are trained in psychotherapy and work with social agencies to support the client's mental and physical well-being. They cannot administer or interpret psychological testing, nor can they prescribe medication.

Culture tends to offer a cumulative wisdom to facilitate and deal with one's psycho-socio-polico-spiritual context successfully. However, cultures too can become confusing and sometimes contaminated due to historical influences and political movements often needing reforms, self-examination, and deceptive remedies such as dowry and caste system etc. among Hindus. Mental health professionals (not religious authorities) have the primary obligation to tease out the therapeutic verses pathological aspects of the culture. They cannot be relevant to the patient, unless they are able to identify the individual's cultural context, concepts, definitions, ideals, and conflict dynamics. For example, Indian husbands often feel sandwiched between the competing demands of their parents and spouses. Muslim patients by and large terminate therapy after a single session as they feel an overwhelming sense of being disloyal to their faith and family. In other words, every culture defines an individuals' personal boundaries, values, and life destinations. The lack of cultural competence on the part of the mental health professionals guarantees clinical failure.

LIMITATIONS OF CONVENTIONAL THERAPY

The main obstacle to widespread mental health treatment throughout the world is *access*. Seeing a therapist in the developed world is costly, and cannot be utilized by most people unless they have insurance. Even if one has insurance, the co-payment is enough to cause insomnia. Psychiatrists are too busy to spare more than ten minutes. Psychologists do not prescribe and now are so busy that they do not schedule for more than 45 minutes. Most social workers are not necessarily clinically versatile enough (in terms of diagnosis or interventions) to meet clinical psychological needs. They too have joined the capitalistic rank of big fees, short sessions, and waiting lists for appointments. Some social workers and therapists can be equally competent, versatile, and great gatekeepers.

In the developing world (or in the developed world, without insurance), the only way to receive mental health therapy is through community health centers that offer mental health services. But even these types of centers are not always available. Their waiting lists are long. At the same time, they are struggling for survival and are dependent on the aid of government or charities.

In essence, all of this means that mental health services are not available for most people. Even if they exist, they are rarely able to accommodate patients at the time of their most critical need. They may expect patients to wait weeks or months and may only be staffed by a part-time psychiatrist and a team of BA/BSW level therapists. Because of overwhelming numbers, these professionals may feel inclined to railroad their clients into group therapy or expect patients to enroll in all-day programs. On the other hand, group therapy sessions can be remarkably useful and inexpensive.

In terms of the process from admission to discharge, the sequence is usually the same, involving a clinical interview, observation, lots of note-taking, examination by a psychiatrist, and a quick prescription of psychotropic medications, followed by periodic visits with the psychologist, social worker, or therapist. This is called an interdisciplinary approach. It is a caste system, and the one on the top gives you the least time and is most difficult to retain. In today's world, it is very difficult to achieve the ideal where the therapist takes his or her time and relates to the patient like a good old country doctor. On the other hand, the profession of mental health has become more

Mental illness is more pervasive than what we would like to accept. It is all around us and does not discriminate whether one is intelligent or intellectually challenged, pretty, simple, rich, poor, a success, a failure, higher or lower caste, male or female, lives in villages or cities, Hindu, Muslim, or Christian. Psychiatrists, psychologists, doctors, politicians, and religious authorities are all vulnerable to mental problems. Unlike in India, many famous Westerners have come out of the closet regarding their mental problems. Stigma, as real it is, has a high cost as it delayed help and treatment. Children, by virtue of their phase of life, can suffer from stress, depression, social phobias, worrying, and self-esteem issues. Similarly, adolescence comes with its own emotional, sexual, social, academic, and peer pressures. Other phases of life, whether adult (Grihastha) or vanaprastha, have the built in challenges of parenting, elderly care, providing, surviving job stress, and health concerns as well as pressure to redefine the purpose and goals of life. Gradual detachment and giving back to society of vanaprastha phase is highly therapeutic. Sanyasa is the only phase where, if one is lucky, one can physically, psychologically, financially, and emotionally walk away and feel "free from it all." Ashrama Vyavastha is a good prophylactic against mental illness (though a not a serious type such as psychosis and bipolar disorder).

proficient and unlike Freudian days, one does not need to be on the couch for five years, five days a week. Weekly sessions are in most cases enough. Often the total treatment may be successful in six to twenty sessions. However, some illnesses are more serious and require regular follow-up for years.

PSYCHIATRIC MEDICATIONS

Psychotropic (Psychiatric Medications) drugs or mental medications are costly in the developed world and beyond the means of most people. As individual medications are rarely prescribed alone and practically never for a few weeks only, costs can quickly add up, especially when one includes the expense of follow-up appointments, blood work, and side-effect monitoring.

Some precautions about medication which should be discussed with patients:
- Medications are not substitutes for good psychotherapy or vice versa.
- Encourage patients to be educated consumers. Advise them not to alter the dosage without consulting with a physician. In case of severe side effects, stop or reduce the dosage or number of medications.
- Advise the patient that this is a trial-and-error process and that they might need to try several medications before finding the one that works.
- Advise the patient that some mental medications take four-to-six weeks to work.
- Let them know that some medications are addictive or can cause side effects. Encourage them to contact you immediately if they experience out-of-the-ordinary symptoms.

Patients need to be knowledgeable about types of drugs and their effects. Here is a list of commonly prescribed categories of drugs and some comments:
- Anti-anxiety/Anxiolytic (addictive): Xanax, Valium, Librium, Klonopin, Ativan, Serax, Tranxene, Atarax, Buspar, Benadryl, Inderal, Tenormin, Catapres, Restoril.
- Antidepressants (not addictive but risk if discontinued abruptly): Paxil, Prozac, Zoloft, Serzone, Effexor, Luvox, Wellbutrin, Desyrel, Sinequan, Elavil, Norpramin, Pamelor, Sinequan, Asendin, Celexa, Lexapro, Remeron, Vivectil, Eldepryl, Tofranil. Note: Some patients do not respond to this class of drugs, and therefore ECT becomes a treatment of last resort. Suicidal patients especially should be hospitalized and closely monitored.

- Anti-Obsession/Compulsion: Selective serotonin re-uptake inhibitor (SSRIs) include Prozac, Zoloft, Paxil, Luvox, and Anafranil. Note: SSRIs are known to address symptoms of anxiety and depression. Sometimes, unpredictably, they may trigger a hypomania phase in a patient. There is no way to know in advance since these same medications are successfully used for bipolar and manic-depressive patients.
- *Psycho-stimulants* (frequently used for ADD/ADHD kids or alerts): Adderall, Ritalin, Cylert, Dexedrine, Strattera, Concerta, Metadata.
- *Mood Stabilizers/Anticonvulsants* (frequently used for Manic Depressive/Bipolar disorder): Depakote, Tegretol, Eskalith/Lithium, Neurontin, Cerebyx, Lamictal, Trileptal, Topamax.
- *Antipsychotic* (schizophrenia, paranoia, schizoaffective, etc.): Risperdal, Haldol, Navane, Prolixin, Stelazine, Loxitane, Trilafon, Moban, Serentil, Clozaril, Mellaril, Thorazine, Abilify, Loxitane, Zyprexa, Geodon.
- *Anti-addiction:* Antabuse, Dolophin, Revex, Narcan, Buprenex.
- *MAO inhibitors. Note:* These are another set of medications that are utilized for OCD and borderline personality disorders. They have to be watched very carefully as consumption of wine and cheese can be lethal while on these medications. Nardil, Parnate, Eldepryl/Carbex.

Reminder: Many non-psychiatric medications have the potential to cause serious mental disorders such as depression, anxiety, and even psychosis. The list is very long, and the consumer has to learn to take full advantage of his neighborhood pharmacist for advice.

Elderly people have to be extra careful and must consult a physician with gerontology expertise. Pregnant women and breastfeeding mothers must also seek expert advice due to the risk of miscarriage, organicity, neonatal side effects like toxicity and withdrawal symptoms, long-term neo-behavioral effects, ADHD, Learning Disabilities, etc. Similarly, an expert must carefully evaluate the use of mental medications with children under six. In the case of adolescents, the risk of overdose or suicide should also be monitored.

It is a good idea to advise patients to refrain from excessive coffee use and cigarette smoking, and to have a regular sleep routine. Patients need to be attentive to side effects and warning signs and to maintain a journal that logs moods and behaviors while on medication.

Self-Help Solutions and Life Stages

For the most part, our emphasis has been on therapeutic solutions to the mental health issues for Diaspora Indians. We'd be remiss if we did not acknowledge that formal treatment is simply not a practical option for many for a number of reasons:

- It is beyond the financial means of all but the middle and upper classes.
- Psychotherapy is seen as culturally a taboo for many Indians.
- There is a dearth of therapists who are qualified to deal with cross-cultural issues.
- Many people live in small villages and remote areas and have no access to mental health services.
- People often lack information on their mental health options.
- Local medical professionals often fail to be gatekeepers either due to lack knowledge, are complacent to refer patient to other specialists, or because they don't have resources for referral.

Beyond the limitations of the traditional therapeutic model is the more fundamental reality that human beings must learn to take care of themselves, without leaning on a therapist or anyone else. The goal of therapy should be to create the conditions of non-dependence or autonomy, allowing the patient to develop the "therapist within."

Wherever one is on the therapeutic journey, there is a plethora of self-help solutions designed to navigate a path from crisis to wholeness.

The purpose of this chapter is threefold:

1. To give an overview of self-help solutions.
2. To outline when they are appropriate and when they are not.
3. To present a model of human development as a means of underscoring how specific self-help solutions can be integrated.

Let us begin by acknowledging the relevance of self-help solutions. We all want and need, if not perfect, at least adequate, precise, no-nonsense answers to the basic problems, dilemmas, and paradoxes experienced in day-to-day life. We cannot afford to run for professional help or to big cities every time there is an emotional overload, minor insomnia, feelings of anxiousness, etc. We do not want to be alone, overwhelmed, or confused in situations of crises. Often a professional or expert assistance is not easy to find or not affordable. Even if it is available, it is often very hard to utilize because of jargon, bureaucracy, loss of privacy, and wrong timing.

Self-help, therefore, becomes essential not only to prevent crises but often to manage day-to-day life and ordinary stresses. Self-help solutions are plentiful. In the United States, there is even a National Mental Health Self-Help Clearinghouse that links individuals to self-help solutions. There are sections in bookstores stocked with books that offer focused solutions to specific problems. These books break down human issues into minute segments, and concentrate mainly on self-esteem, assertiveness, anger management, guilt dissipation, loving self, codependency, relationship issues, etc. The internet has made it easy to research, self-diagnose, and learn about treatment options.

Almost all developed countries have professional associations, organizations, and societies that provide initial guidance and referrals. Often there are foundations specializing in different disorders that can provide handouts, fliers, and other supplies. In the US, there is even an Alliance for Mentally Ill (NAMI), which provides self-help resources to patients and their families. Developing countries are still lacking the wherewithal to cope with people's need for self-help materials.

In addition to books, there are support groups for people with conditions that range from migraine to menopause and bipolar disorder to baldness. There are workshops or process initiatives, such as the Erhard Seminar Training (EST) and its offshoots, that seek to offer participants catharsis after a three-to-five day experience. There are companies, such as Sounds True which sell motivational tools in the form of CDs, DVDs or mp3s. Yoga classes and similar groups are commonplace nowadays, and these are a powerful means for stress prevention and management.

Unlike Alcoholics Anonymous or its offspring, where the emphasis is surrendering to the group philosophy, the focus of many of these tools or processes is self-direction. When they succeed, it is because they offer replicable structures, routines, and value systems that match user needs. When they do not succeed, it may be because they fail to instill motivation in users or because there may be a mismatch between what they purport to offer and user needs. They may also have limited utility for those who have serious emotional disorders and may be in need of more formal and a more sustained, therapeutic approach.

A truly holistic approach would recognize that there is a continuum that encompasses therapeutic and self-help approaches. The core beliefs of the self-help movement–taking charge of one's self-care, perfecting self-empowerment, changing lifestyles, utilizing what's useful from Eastern wisdom or Western techniques– are all positive. For the most part, the mental health system has not taken advantage of what is useful in these approaches. More importantly, the mental health system does not adequately prepare patients for life after therapy when self-help technologies might provide useful support.

LIMITATIONS OF SELF-HELP SOLUTIONS

For mild to moderate mental health issues, self-help therapy undoubtedly has several advantages over traditional face-to-face therapy. The do-it-yourself approach is convenient, cheap, and can be pursued at the patient's pace. For moderate-to-severe mental health issues, however, there are significant disadvantages:

- You may lack the perspective to understand properly the nature of your issues. Your ability to help yourself will only be as good as your ability to be objective and clear about what the nature of your issues is.

- You may lack the knowledge of how to fix your issues. Even if you can be objective and accurate about the nature of your issues, you are still faced with the challenge of figuring out how to solve them.
- You may lack the motivation or willpower to stick to a self-help plan. Even if you know what to do to solve your problem, you aren't always able to stick to your plan and follow through well enough to benefit from your plan.

INTERLUDE: SELF-HELP APHORISMS

- There is no perpetual happiness. Stress, pain, suffering, hurt, and let downs are waiting just around the corner.
- Death is inevitable and so is aging. Fear of death, uncertainty, and not knowing causes panic in most people.
- Relationships are never perpetually peaceful. One cannot live with them or without them.
- Free will is an illusion since responsibilities, obligations, the needs of significant others, and social interactions entangle us in the roller coaster, i.e. business of living day-to-day.
- Life is risky, and it does not come with a fail-proof warranty.
- It is an unmistakable fact that every action has a consequence.
- One can plan but what actually happens is an entirely different matter. One still has to act as if one is in charge and has a destination.

STAGES OF LIFE: FOUNDATION FOR SELF-HELP

Self-help implies proactively managing healthy, balanced lifestyle and integrate somato-psycho-socio-spiritual aspects of living. Self-help does not mean avoiding mental health services but simply taking personal responsibility. It requires conceptual clarity as to the phases/stages of life. With a model of human phases, one can anticipate, prepare, and accomplish what must be done and how to do it. Every journey requires an itinerary.

One of the Western models was developed by American psychologist Eric Erikson, who postulated that humans undergo eight stages of development. Erickson believed that people experience conflicts that serve as turning points. These conflicts are centered on either developing or failing to develop a particular psychological transaction.

For example, the sixth stage of psychosocial development occurs during early adulthood and is characterized by reconciling issues of intimacy versus isolation. According to Erickson's theory, people who were successful during this stage were able to develop intimate and committed relationships. Those who were not successful were more likely to suffer emotional isolation, loneliness, and depression.

Although Erickson's theory holds merit, author favors Ashram Vyavastha-4 phases as prescribed in Hindu psychology. Hindu model incorporate psycho-somato-socio-spiritualistic holism; prescriptions for each phase of life from birth to death. These ashramas lay out a comprehensive description of challenges and solutions but most importantly define the purpose of every stage. As a result, there is no reason to feel lost, purposeless or disconnected which is a major epidemic in the West necessitating formal psychotherapy.

The first phase of life, which ranges from age twelve to twenty-five, is Brahmacharya. This phase requires celibacy, perfecting physical health, developing moral character, learning to respect others, sacrificing personal pleasures, and prioritizing being a student and acquiring wisdom. Unlike in the West, the young are required to sublimate their sexuality, hedonism, and materialism in favor of cultivating exceptional character and relinquishing ego. This approach prevents unnecessary distractions, destructive experimentation and removes all stress to prematurely declare manhood or womanhood. The senses are harnessed for the higher cause of preparing for the next phase of the rest of one's life.

Ancient Hindu psychologist understood the power and the necessity of sublimation. Learning in the Hindu tradition is not just gathering information to become financially independent, get a job, or obtain economic prosperity. It is not just about learning how to drive a car, rent an apartment, or manage finances. Instead, it is about the pursuit of wisdom. Pleasure, comfort, distraction, and sexuality are prohibited in favor of sublimation. Instead, one learns the art and skills of self-management. Learning to convert raw energy, impulses, and desires into socially constructive outlets cannot be deferred until adulthood and also cannot be suddenly integrated during the elderly years. Successful sublimation is a lifelong process; the earlier one starts, the greater the possibility of realizing one's maximum potential.

For child psychology, this implies not pressuring the child to rush prematurely into growing up. He is to remain in "carefree child mode" for an extended period and surrender individuality to the hierarchy of elders, family, and community. Cleverness, manipulation, self-centeredness, selfishness, arrogance, argumentativeness, defiance, indulgence through negatives behaviors like sex, drugs, and cigarettes are taboo. This is the blueprint the child, adolescent, and young adult is expected to follow for his first twenty-five years. He is not allowed to be motivated by money or seek possessions, become a consumer, or a materialistic being.

The second phase, Grihastha, covers the period of the next 25 years, until age 50. This is the ideal age range, but the actual time period depends on life circumstances. For example, if the family has no breadwinner, then it is incumbent upon the young to sacrifice education and be the provider. Or, he might in other circumstances marry at a younger age for family reasons. Respect, obedience, responsibility, and sacrifice are among the essential ingredients of Hindu vocabulary.

Grihastha Ashrama recognizes humans' biological, psychological, and social needs. That includes engaging in sexual pleasure in marriage, procreation, practicing one's profession, earning and accumulating wealth. It also recognizes that elders and parents must be cared for and provided for at the same time one provides for one's own children. In Hindu culture, it is thus rather common that three generations live together as an extended or joint family. This often includes siblings and their families. The Hindu family operates like a clan and a battalion where every member has a defined place, role, duty, obligations and status.

The family is the nucleus of the larger society. Its role is not limited to bearing and rearing children, but to providing a foundation and structure so individuals can learn to coexist, appreciate and role model as to their duties before rushing to any separation-individuation i.e. Consumerism and materialism. Householder stage is viewed as the toughest, most crucial phase due to polarizing demand of various role, expectations and personal sacrifice. Grihastha Ashram, therefore presents the greatest challenge and opportunity to grow. It tests an individual's endurance, resilience, and preparedness. Fortunately, the proverb, "It takes a village to raise a child," is living proof in Hindu society.

Grihastha Ashram, is the only phase which allows sexual pleasures/hedonism/ materialism. The break for individuation and separation does not come until the next phase and that too only if one has fulfilled all obligations required/prescribed for the second phase. Prescribed 25 years may not be long enough to meet all the expectations and, therefore, Grihastha may need to be extended. It is believed that premature rushing to the next stage will result in corrupt behavior due to not having fulfilled all sexual, etc. needs.

The next (third) phase of Vanaprastha brings back the need to refocus on sublimation; this time more on social service. One cannot enter into it unless one is ready to take the sublimation to a higher level of transcendence: the pursuit of serving (Nishkam Sewa) the larger society and spirituality without any personal gain, fame or return. The risk of becoming corrupt, deviant, or sociopathic is much higher if one has not gone through the nitty-gritty experiences of the Grihastha phase. Here, sublimation demands absolute self-discipline of thought, feelings, motivational clarity, emotional neutrality, and maximum simplicity. The process of sublimation can be defined as mindfully redirecting raw energy, (aggression, sexuality, attachments, possessions, identifications, desires, fear, instincts, and impulses) into refined thoughts, feelings and actions which will nurture, support, and benefit the larger society. Every aspect of Hindu Dharma is geared toward this single goal from birth to death; freedom from ignorance, suffering and being recycled.

It's paradoxical that decision-making is influenced by emotions and vice versa. Ideally, it should be based on the ability to integrate the maximum possible variables one can imagine. In reality, decisions are based on stress, threats, demands, compulsions, desires, impulses, duty, needs, and wants. The most important considerations in decision-making one has to take are independence from others and balancing conflicting demands, hopefully with a clear understanding of the larger context. Hindu personality tends to struggle between duty, others' expectations, and at the cost of self, autonomy, and feelings. If decision-making feels overwhelming or ambivalence dominates the choices, then it's time to seek psychological counseling. A proactive approach has the potential to minimize damage and emotional suffering. To learn, improve, or make better decisions is one of the reasons individuals consult mental health professionals.

Vanaprastha Ashram extends for 25 years ranging from ages 51 to 76. In Sanskrit, Vanaprastha literally means departure for the jungle or retiring to the forest. "Jungle" is a metaphor for taking inventory of personal dharma, solitude, detachment, disengagement and relinquishing "I", "me" and "mine." When one is ready to let go of one's ego, one can truly become free even before death. In Hindu psychology, Ego is viewed as the source of ignorance, ignorance as the source of confusion and in turn reason for most suffering. Many diseases have more to do with chemistry, genetics and environment and not ego or karma. Ego is viewed as inseparable from materialism, personal identity and individuality, as it is prevalent in the West. To retain or embrace ego and to operate from it is sheer masochism and spiritual suicide as per Hindu psychology.

The Vanaprastha phase, in a superficial way, is similar to retirement in the West. Unlike retirement in the capitalistic society, the Vanaprastha person does not seek engagement or spend his lifelong acquired wisdom in playing golf or bingo, pursuing hobbies, babysitting, or returning to part-time earning.

The final phase is Sanyasa, or renunciation. This last stage extends until death (ideally to age 100), with the focus being on total resignation, detachment from family, society, money, sex, and desires. This is accomplished by giving up one's birth name, religious identity, titles, affiliations and all possessions. By relinquishing one's familiar psychological identity, one can then leisurely and fully devote one's energy to either pursuing Nirvana or social service (nishkaam seva) with no barriers and burdens.

Sankhya-Yoga school is one of the six systems of Indian psychology, the goal in essence being internal and interpersonal harmony and creating a context for the realization of one's total potential. Sankhya is the theory of yoga while yoga is the practice of Sankhya. It consists of eight steps: Yama, Niyama, Asana, Pranayama, Prityahara, Dharna, Dhyan, and Samadhi. Yama to Dhyan have direct relevance to managing mind, body, and behavior. They're relevant to not only preventing physical or emotional distress but also facilitating happiness. The last step of Samadhi is expected to lead to Moksha or freedom from the cycle of birth and death. Regular practice of Sankhya Yoga is a powerful tool for self-help, not only during Sanyasa but through all stages of life. Variants of this practice are becoming mainstream all over the world and are being utilized by organizations including schools, governments, corporations, and the military.

SELF-HELP TECHNIQUES

- *Self-Discipline*. self-help is not merely thinking about it, having clear concepts but also practicing in behavior while surrendering feelings/self-doubts, confusion, illusions, laziness and rationalizations. There is no magic that can guarantee happiness. Self-discipline is a prerequisite. Usually, it takes about 90 days for a disciplined practice to become a habit.
- *Samkalpa*. A samkalpa is a resolve. It is an affirmation that is made to overcome any weakness affecting body, performance,

and life, and to awaken any other strength to provide internal balance. These are short sentences that one can use to program the subconscious mind in a particular positive direction. Samkalpas can be stated before a particular practice (such as yoga), during weakness or illness, or throughout the day. Regular practice can help focus direction, fend off distractions, and enhance decision-making and planning.

- *Fasting.* To fast is to give the mind and body a break from thinking and feeling related overload. Constant consumption or sensory interaction is not only disruptive and stressful but potentially addictive to the stimuli. Absence of such stimuli can result in boredom, irrationally acting out, or simply withdrawal. Fasting can reset the circuits and help the body and mind decrease its dependence on stimuli. This can be mental fasting, involving the practice of silence and avoiding stimuli such as television and texting, or physical fasting i.e, refraining from the consumption of food. Individuals suffering from serious illness such as diabetes should consult their physician before practicing physical fasting.

- *Relaxation.* To manage one's sympathetic nervous system, arousal, sensory excitement, and emotional overload, one needs to practice relaxation. Relaxation can be practiced through simple means, such as simply being quiet and refraining from distractions. However, utilizing food, alcohol, smoking, drug use, or sex as a means of bringing about relaxation is harmful and counterproductive.

- *Cognitive Restructuring.* An undisciplined mind, if not managed, can wreak havoc on thoughts, feelings, and behavior. Meditation, mantra, and breathing exercises can be useful in disciplining the mind. These practices can be combined with fasting and other techniques.

- *Living in the Moment.* Everything happens in the context of time. It is crucial to be able to balance preoccupation with the past and projections about the future by simply surrendering and being in the moment. Breathing exercises and meditation are the most powerful techniques that can help one live in the moment.

- *Practicing Rituals.* Observing rituals, such as participating in pilgrimages, community celebrations, or practicing pooja (a Hindu offering to various deities, distinguished persons, or special guests), can be very therapeutic. One can also make one's own rituals to neutralize stress. People in Western countries use "Happy Hour" as a time to let go of stress, but, of course, this revolves around alcohol. But there is no reason one can't create one's own "Happy Hour" ritual that does not involve alcohol.

BRAHMACHARYA: SOME CHALLENGES

It is not easy to be different when others/peers are living impulsively, engaging in sex, using drugs, smoking cigarettes, etc. Particularly when living in foreign societies, to go against the tide is very challenging. It is doable and will require conscious juggling to manage two worlds; one expected by family and other expected by pers. Parents should understand the child/adolescent's stresses /dilemmas and provide personal or professional assistance.

- Drug use among young children is more common than is realized.
- For a child, separations, divorces, relocations, abrupt changes, marital conflicts, domestic violence, financial insecurities, and obsession for money or material things can cause significant stress.
- Mood disorders like depressions and bipolar disorder are starting earlier among children. Mood disorders may appear as problems at school or sudden defiance and violence. They also may be brought on by drug or alcohol use.
- See children's conduct-related problems, oppositional behavior, personality changes, explosive episodes, class disruptive behavior, obsessive, compulsive, and ritualistic behavior as warning signs and do not ignore or minimize them.

- Children's stress can be lowered or alleviated by adjusting parent expectations, limiting choices, and establishing a consistent routine and structure. It is often harmful to enroll a child in too many activities. "Keep it simple, stupid," as they say in Alcohol Anonymous.
- Parents should discourage materialistic values, sexuality, and exposure to violence. Parents can do their child a service early on by introducing the idea of globalization and promoting interest in the world. This can be done through encouraging the learning of a foreign language, or helping develop an interest in other cultures. Instead of taking children instinctively to fast food restaurants, take them instead to ethnic restaurants, neighborhoods, and markets.
- Live life and do not make children the center of your world. Kids do not need to be made princes and princesses, told every five minutes that they are loved, are good, and can become anything they want to be. The reality is they have to learn to share space and things, make sacrifices, practice living by the family schedule, and enjoy and play with simple things.
- Children are allergic to religion. Do not shove it down their throats. Present it as entertainment and opportunity to become a specialist. In time, they will learn to make sound choices. There are other things you can teach to inspire your children to be good human beings. Introduce collectivism rather than individualism, downplay materialism, and emphasize giving over taking and contentment with what they have over making the Christmas list.

The schooling phase has become unusually stressful for children, families, and teachers. Parents have become neurotic not only due to the pressure of working but because of self-doubt about their parenting skills. They fear that they have caused or will cause damage to their kids. They also fear that they will never turn out to be good enough parents, or anticipate that their kids will have low self-esteem, will not be well rounded, or will end up using drugs. Teachers are overwhelmed because they are not allowed to be teachers but are expected to act as self-esteem builders, babysitters, diagnosticians, therapists, and peacemakers. Everyone is sandwiched and overwhelmed and, in the final analysis, children lose.

Each child is uniquely individual and has different limitations, resources and, in essence, unique personalities. Unlike robots, they follow their own pace and creative instincts. Some are gifted, others are challenged, and the rest fall in-between. They can also be handicapped, troubled, or just outright emotionally impaired. Parental openness, readiness, and empathy become vital, as is the need to seek interdisciplinary evaluations, procure adequate help, and adjust expectations. Parents need not act as adversaries to the school, specialists, and mental health professionals. It never hurts to seek many opinions, ask questions, and persevere until questions are answered, solutions or limitations are identified, and necessary resources are found. If parents feel ambivalent, or overwhelmed during the process, they must seek out counseling for themselves.

Treatment options and systems are rapidly evolving. Professionals are becoming more refined. And the research is leading towards new solutions almost yearly. Therefore, the parental approach has to be one of working as a team and relinquishing unnecessary paranoia, fear, and intensity. They can start the process by self-help reading, Internet research, talking to the child's pediatrician, teacher, and counselor or calling their state or national psychology associations.

Students with special needs may require to see a school psychologist, social worker, learning consultant, audiologist, speech therapist, an internist, neurologist, ophthalmologist, a psychiatrist, or a combination there of. Comprehensive evaluations are essential to finding the right solutions. Parents can initiate such requests.

There are several signs that indicate the need for early evaluations. Warning signs include sudden onset of impulsivity, hyperactivity, impaired attention, acting violently or self-destructively, behaving in a detached and self-preoccupied manner, and falling behind peers in school. Other early indicators are a child's inability to organize and follow age-appropriate instructions, inability to understand what parents and the teacher are saying, forgetfulness, insomnia, nightmares, sleep walking, sudden defiance, stealing, and the inability to care for self.

Do not delay or waste time thinking he will outgrow these behaviors, worrying about social stigma that the child will be labeled, or that you will face embarrassment. It's not about you but your child's long-term future. The best place to start is to make a file. Start observing and noting problem behaviors. Before seeing a professional, make sure you bring comprehensive information, including the mother's health during pregnancy, delivery, developmental milestones, history of diseases, hospitalization, injuries, medicines, and a list of names and addresses of other doctors.

Every time you see a professional, retain their business card and a copy of their reports in the file. Good records make it easier for a professional to see the bigger picture. Be sure to let the professional know if there are marital conflicts, spousal abuse, alcohol addiction, or any change in the family situation such as relocations or deaths. While waiting to see a professional, try hard to make sure the child is not doing drugs, being abused or traumatized, and that he is not experiencing sight, hearing, or speech impairments, or using medications which may be causing sluggishness or lethargy.

VANAPRASTHA: AN ALTERNATIVE TO WESTERN RETIREMENT

The Western motto of living is to be productive and engagement till the end.. As a result, work and what one does for a living becomes a central theme of one's life. Hindu psychology emphasizes disengagement and total relinquishing. For Indians, work is what one does, and it is not the essence of one's life. For example, most Indian parents do not encourage their children to work or earn while studying. In their minds, being a student is "all or nothing". They see earning/working as a distraction. Similarly, during the Marital/Householder phase, Hindus see working, earning, providing, and raising a family. as essential priorities. In the Vanaprastha phase, an Indian is ideally preparing himself for a gradual disengagement, and detachment from identity that was based on ego, attachments and possessions. The psychological journeys to reinvent oneself and to explore new and creative ways to sublimate become essential. It is part of the mental hygiene and cultural prescription. In the West, there is no pressure to detach, relinquish and distance oneself. Existing on the margins of the rat race is acceptable. For Hindus, nothing is without spirituality, and spirituality is nothing without relinquishing it all.

> *"It is the nature of desire never to be fulfilled, but he who eternally gives it up is eternally fulfilled at that very moment."*
> Tirukural 370

VANAPRASTHA VS. RETIREMENT

- In the Western lifestyle/culture, retirement simply means to let go the same old routine and to give priority to what gives one pleasure. The self-focus becomes important. Continued consumption remains the drive of human behavior. Spirituality is mistakenly seen as synonymous to religion. In essence, one continues to psychologically, emotionally, socially and financially remain being recycled in the same old rut but simply more time at hand. Vanaprastha is in juxtaposition.

- Insecurity, worrying, fear and constant pressure to keep up with daily challenges tends to be a full-time job in the Western context. Westerners always seem to be short on time and constantly negotiating priorities. Vanaprastha allows one to feel free, live simple, and pursue service.

- The Western context requires sense-based interaction and

existence. Reality is dominated by what one sees, feels, hears, tastes, thinks, or anticipates. Vanaprastha can successfully facilitate intuition-based living and meditation-based experiences. Sensory-based living tends to be reactive, leaving the sympathetic nervous system exhausted. The Vanaprasthee learns to live through the parasympathetic nervous system, non-reactivity, detached action, and emotional neutrality. There is nothing to control, nobody to impress and no hidden agenda nor need for an ulterior motive. One does not have to do more or try harder, but merely allow life to happen.

- Unlike the Western push to change things, improve the surrounding milieu, pursue bigger, better and more, in Vanaprastha one can choose to become free from possessions, desires, and narrow parochial loyalties. One can start preparing or living for what one always wanted to do – be free. Detachment, contentment and visualizing the state of being in nothingness are powerful concepts to promote ultimate well-being.

- If one never had a happy place, happy phase, or happy time, the Vanaprastha gives a last chance to reexamine it all and start afresh. It frees us from the obligation to be needed, approved, or defined. It allows one to begin laying the groundwork for freedom.

- In Vanaprastha, one gets a chance to redefine the meaning, purpose, direction, priorities, self, others, and even religiosity. One is permitted to shrug off the old and resume a new identity or even relinquish all given or chosen identities.

- Vanaprastha is synonymous with making a difference internally or externally, personally or socially, resigning or restarting, and even all at once. There is no place for the status quo, stagnation, or just getting by. Vanaprastha offers the opportunity and means to rise above the mundane.

- The midpoint in life does not have to be midlife crises. With some awareness and realization, it can be a high time for sublimation. Sexuality has to be put in its proper place around this time since it offers a rather limited means to become intimate and experience joy. The desires will only lead to frustration and, therefore, one needs to be open to experience a higher level of maturity, not based on the senses but rather on consciousness, balance, and mindfulness.

- One can afford to become the roving ambassador of service and good will by visiting various countries and attempting to make the world a better place than when first encountered.

VANAPRASTHA: CHALLANGES

- Worldly people and places where all the economic, social, and emotional drama takes place are not favorable to Vanaprastha. The rat race is nothing but a sympathetic nervous system roller coaster that is tied to negative feelings and stress. The Grihastha period has lasted 25 years, and that should be enough to make one tired of experiencing stress. Distance from the familiar and routine places such as family, work, business, and socialization is required. Interacting in the society in which one lived his or her earlier phases must be curtailed significantly. If one desires less or, even better, nothing, the potential for contentment increases multi-fold. Desire is the single most threatening element as it triggers the entire somato-psycho-socio-spiritual crisis (vicious cycle of like-dislike, clinging-aversion, pleasure-pain, etc.). As long as one pursues people, things, objects, and stimuli and experiences, one is doomed to suffer from the endless chain of insecurity, depression, vulnerability, anxiety, worrying, and obsessing.
- If necessary, one can return to the household one left behind from time-to-time. One can even relinquish Vanaprastha and return to one's place in the family, work, and society.
- The wife may accompany the husband in Vanaprastha and with him follow the same routine. The sexual dimension of the relationship must be moderated but not given up as in the final phase, Sanyasa.

- Fancy clothes, costly fabric, and customized tailoring must be avoided. Clothes should be made of vegetable fibers, honoring simplicity and autonomy. Nature was our original home and now we get another chance to return to it.

- Food should be vegetarian, simple, mostly consisting of plants, fruits, and vegetables. One should consume one meal a day, never completely filling the stomach. One must make sure, before eating, that no one in sight is hungry. It is one's duty to invite a hungry person, whether friend or foe. Alcohol and drugs are an absolute taboo in Vanaprastha.

- Meditation, contemplation, good reading, and yoga should occupy all available leisure time. However, gardening is not prohibited.

- Adequate time should be spent teaching, helping, supporting, and nurturing others in hospitals, schools, orphanages, and other appropriate social service settings. Attaching to a temple to offer specialized services is also recommended.

- Serving society is the most important mission along with meditation, contemplation, silence, and acquiring knowledge. Ritual participation is deemphasized.

- Possessiveness for land, gold and the opposite sex has to be avoided. Ambition, desire, honors, wealth, and luxury must be curtailed. All nonessential money matters must be restricted.

- Frugality, simplicity, and contentment are essential traits to be practiced.

- Restraining anger, relinquishing pride and subordinating all negative feelings are essential in the Vanaprastha life. Buddha viewed anger as one of the three poisons along with greed and delusion. Non-reactivity is the ultimate strength of a model Vanaprasthee. Detaching from anger holds the key. Emotions of compassion and equanimity are cultivated.

Towards a Cross-Cultural Psychology

Man and culture are inseparable. People change depending upon changes in the social milieu but the core often remains rather deeply entrenched and influencing perceptions, thinking, feeling and behavior. East and west are different but twins have started to meet more in specific contexts. Globalization, Americanization, pervasiveness of capitalistic style materialism has significantly impacted human behavior even in the remotest part of the world. American standard and expectations have become the baseline and the desired goals. However, the context of one's core culture continues to dictate their perception of self, others, the world, and practice of faith, preference for music, food and lifestyle.

When one refers to personality, mental health, mental disorders and psychological treatment, they are highly culture specific. We live our concepts and they evolve in the context of one's past, religion, culture, ethnicity and early psycho-social milieu. West defines ego as executive functioning of the mind while Hindus as "I", "me" and "mine" i.e. Pathological. Westerners promote separation-individuation/autonomy of the child while easterners nurture dependence, collectivism and loyalty. In essence, in spite of overt verbalizations and resemblances, the core character of the person is highly culturally determined.

Therefore, approaching the mental disorder diagnosis, and treatment must be processed thru the cross cultural perspective. In essence, all psychology has to be culturally congruent and personally relevant. There is no one fit for all. In other words, Hindu Psychology is clinically rich and has vast variety of procedures which can be very cost effective. However, it does not mean that modern medicine and crisis management should not be open for integration.

These self-help procedures are part of everyday living. Moreover, the Eastern languages, in particular, Sanskrit, Hindi and other provincial languages have concepts that are meaningful to facilitate therapy. For example, Happiness is defined not as sense based gratification but more as contentment. Non-injury, emotional equanimity are other concepts utilized to manage overload of feelings. Until recently, Globalization has some negative implications i.e. Indians did not have terms for panic, depression, post trauma, etc. but now it has become part of everyday lingo. Indian practically never used the word depression but only sad. The concept of depression now has become universal similar to panic, post trauma, etc.

The principle reasons for Western psychology to evolve the way it has are rooted in its Eurocentric history, culture, politics, two World Wars and related post World War chaos, destruction, and dislocations. Thinkers like Freud, Adler, Sullivan, Jung, etc. struggled with their Judeo-Christian-guilt context as well as their nuclear personal and family dynamics. Their projections and interpretations became the foundation of Western psychology. It is, however, important to note that Western psychology since then has evolved, diversified and made tremendous strides to become universally applicable to a large extent. Eclectic approaches blending best of the both worlds is the call of the 21st century..

THE HISTORY OF WESTERN PSYCHOTHERAPY

Western psychology has a very short history of roughly about 100 years. Its origin can be traced to Germany, specifically and Europe generally. It is ethnic i.e. Caucasian in its roots. As a consequence, Caucasian, European mindset, definitions, concepts dominate defining the personality, interpersonal relationships and behavioral patterns. Its highly Greek, Jewish and Victorian in its culture. By implication, it is limited and incongruent to the personal and interpersonal dynamics of individuals from other continents, cultures, religions, and societies. India's Hindu culture and Middle Eastern Muslim cultures are a good examples of Eurocentric psychology's incongruence and incompatibility ranging from perceptions to concepts.

As it speedily evolved in the West, psychology was a by-product of the two World Wars. In essence, it has its origin in crisis, violence (aggression), distrust, struggle for survival, avoidance of alienation, and reclaiming one's identity. Obviously, two world wars had created significant disruptions of the family and in social, economic, and even religious aspects of the society. Western psychology evolved to meet these challenges not only by developing European concepts such as identity, individuality, separation, and individuation but also by providing clinical procedures to address neurosis, psychosis, acting out, depression, panic, and phobias. It's an indicative of a psychology in response to holocaust. Although it has made great strides, Western psychology has limitations that to a great extent stem from its early founders' attempts to establish it as a rigorously scientific field, akin to biology and physics.

Among these limitations:
- *Reductionism* or dissecting the human experience into separate parts, such as Id, Ego, Superego, Child, Adult, and Parent. Treating a human as the sum of its disparate parts is not adequate to describe the totality of the human essence.
- *An overemphasis on defense mechanisms.* These are often crudely viewed as the only mechanisms that sustain the human mind. But it is a mistake to view defense mechanisms as the sole and primary drivers of human experience. Hindu culture presents an alternative approach that emphasizes disengagement, detachment, and relinquishing control.
- *The cult of the individual.* The individual is given the central role, and thus his/her and I/Me/Mine become the primary frame of reference. This leads to "You and I," "Yours and Mine," and "I am for me and I need to make sure I am in

control, so you don't come to grab what is mine." The implication is that I have to be alert, vigilant, powerful, assertive, protective and defensive, i.e., to exist in a survival mode. By contrast, the Hindu approach takes the survival mode for granted and is more preoccupied with rising above the mundane and the ordinary.

- *Defining reality as something concrete.* Reality in the West is defined as something very concrete and to be taken with the utmost seriousness. An alternate approach is to define this reality as illusory, transitory, perpetually reshaping, and therefore not worthy of attachment or seriousness.

- *An overemphasis on autonomy.* The Western goal in life is to master the environment, ensure physical survival and develop personal competence to meet individual needs. Western values are autonomy, personal space, and processing reality via the senses. Easterners, in general, are more collective-oriented and value the needs of the extended family over those of the individual.

- *The primacy of feelings.* To the Western mind, feelings are the primary means to experience the self, the other, the external world, and everything else. The Eastern mind sees feelings as the ultimate barriers to becoming truly objective, neutral, and free from it all.

- *Action/Reaction.* The Western mind deals with stimulation by responding to it and perfecting a strategy to balance it. An alternate approach is to practice non-reaction, and thus avoid the formation of habits that stem from reactions to stimuli. We all know that modern day psychologists make their living by helping people deal with their bad habits. Capitalism needs people to have habits, so they remain consumers. Keeping consumers in the perpetual crisis of needing more keeps the economy going. Every product becomes tied to ego, self-esteem, neediness, and "success."

OPPOSITES OF WESTERN & EASTERN ORIENTATION

Western psychologists who treat patients from the East need to keep in mind the differences between their own perspective and that of their patients.

Western	Eastern
Fight or flight	Non-reactivity
Processing of hearing, seeing, tasting and smelling	Turning off the senses
Stimuli dependence	Emotional equanimity
Arousal/sensory basis	Letting it pass
Externally driven/dependent	Silent inward focus
Emphasis on talking	Fasting from speaking
Need to be logical	Experiencing the experience
Perfection of defense mechanisms	Stripping oneself of all defenses, even ego
Goal directed	Focused on here and now
Happiness in sensory gratification	Contentment, equilibrium of mind-body by detachment
Active action, decision	Quiet, passivity, inner reflection
Focused on being productive and accomplished	Focused on just being in the state of surrender
Emphasis on materialism	Detachment from possessions
Stress is normal & a prerequisite to being alive	Stress is an indicator pathology i.e. reactivity
Proactive Problem-solving	Quieting the mind
Senses and logic define reality	The only reality is there is no reality
Mind is the seat of control	Mind is a servant of the senses
Control is essential	Controlling is a burden

Satisfaction of Desires is ok.	Giving in to desires triggers suffering
Emotions are important	Emotions are a burden and must be sublimated at all cost
Individual responsibility	Collective responsibility
Individual needs are most important	Individual needs are subordinate to family and significant others
Identity is a result of trial and error	Identity evolves by role modeling and passing through critical phases
Emphasis on nuclear family	Extended family loyalty
Logic and rationality are emphasized	Intuition and instinct are nurtured
Emotions are to be dealt with pragmatically	Emotions must be sacrificed for duty and obligations
Play, leisure are important and acceptable	No concept of work and play or leisure time.
Time is counted in terms of accomplishments	Time is viewed as circular and not to be taken seriously
Individual freedom of choice	Choices are predetermined by larger family needs and responsibility
Individual is empowered to making things happen	Things/events are destined
Guilt for personal failure	Failure not guilt is a motivator
World is viewed as real and "one life to live"	World is viewed as transitory, perpetual & an illusion
Hypocrisy/contradictions are result in emotional distress	It's all seen as a paradox. Hypocrisy does not create neurosis
Reality is sense-based	Sense-based "reality" is non-reality

When treating an Indian patient, it's helpful to use concepts of Indian culture, that builds on the rich psychological traditions of India as captured in the indigenous texts such as The Upanishads and the philosophical schools of Vedānta, Sāṁkhya, Yoga, Nyāya, Vaiśeṣika and dissenting systems like Jainism and Buddhism. They should not be mistaken for religions but seen as pre-European psychologies.

VEDIC PSYCHOLOGY

Vedic psychotherapy embodies the oldest known clinical procedures used to help human beings deal with their feelings as well as the dilemmas of life, death, growth, and Nirvana (liberation). While aspects of Vedic psychology have been incorporated by Western schools of psychotherapy, its essence is fundamentally different. For example, its closest Western counterparts–Rational-Emotive Therapy (RET), Cognitive Behavioral Therapy (CBT), and Behavior Modification–have a single-minded focus. In contrast, Vedic psychotherapy holistically addresses cognitive restructuring, habit modifications and behavior personality transformation and integration of spirituality.

There are five specific goals in the practice of Vedic psychotherapy:
1. Because most emotional problems correlate with the *tamasik* (impulsive, short-sighted, and self-centered) and *rajasik* (materialistic, and pleasure-oriented) traits of personality, a fundamental goal is to help the person to develop a *satvik* disposition rooted in the search for mindful living, individual-social, internal-external harmony, and the pursuit of spirituality.
2. The philosophy of *Sankhya* (described below) is introduced as a means of promoting conceptual understanding, mind management, body control, cognitive restructuring, habit

cessation, and managing day-to-day life situations proactively without reactivity.

3. Yoga techniques are taught to integrate the mind and body, the internal with the external, the physical and the spiritual. The usual positive side effects of engaging in Sankhya Yoga include SNS-PSNS control, freedom from struggle, pain, and doom-gloom.

4. The concept of the four Ashrams (stages of life) is introduced earlier are a framework for recognizing, labeling, organizing and facing life's demands, responsibilities, and priorities.

5. The psychology of desires and the dynamics behind the dance of incompatible opposites cause roller coaster of thinking an feelings. The necessity and the skills of sublimation are taught to turn the perpetual highs and lows, pain-pleasure, boredom-excitement, and action-reaction vicious cycles into living a life of meaning, purpose, and self-actualization. Learning to overcome negative emotions like anxiety, worrying, fear, anger, sadness, and jealousy are addressed via value clarification, conceptual restructuring, self-confrontation, where higher purposes and spirituality are pursued. In other words, sublimation and emotional equanimity become important steps for self-help and personal transformation.

ESSENTIAL CONCEPTS IN VEDIC PSYCHOTHERAPY

Sankhya-Yoga is the school of philosophical psychology founded by Maharishi Patanjali, who compiled the Yoga Sutras approximately two hundred years before the birth of Christ. Sankhya is the theory of Yoga and Yoga is the practice of Sankhya. Without the theory, practice alone is inadequate; without practice, the theory is inadequate. Yoga follows the eight steps of *Yama* (regulations to control and discipline the lower instincts in human beings), *Niyama* (observances which help to develop a cultured and civilized life), Asana (yogic exercises and postures), Pranayama (the art of regulating the breathing), Prityahara (process of negation), Dharna Dhyan (Meditation), and Samadhi (deep meditation).

Ashram. As discussed earlier, Hinduism prescribes four phases or Ashrams as a schedule of life: Brahmacharya (period of student life and learning), Grihastha (period of householder), Vanaprastha (period for giving back to society and related social welfare activities), and Sanyasa (period of renunciation).

Personality. Each individual has a unique constellation of traits. However, each personality has a preponderance of specific traits:

The Tamasik person is impulsive, short-sighted, and self-centered. In Western psychology, such a personality is labeled antisocial and narcissistic. A person who has a Tamasik personality is a concrete person, governed by basic biological needs, indulging in eating meat and using alcohol. He is not simply a non-vegetarian but prefers the sour taste and leftover food.

Rajasik personality traits are preponderantly hedonistic, materialistic, and pleasure-oriented. However, the person with this personality would also be more resourceful and insightful than the Tamasik person.

The Satvik, in essence, means the procedures for mastering sympathetic nervous system from controlling the body and mind. Satvik Personality is consciously organized around becoming free from the perpetual yo-yo dance between the sympathetic and parasympathetic nervous systems. Satvikta is the pursuit of spirituality, by using body-mind-self as an instrument for personal transformation. Identity for a wise person is not gender, ethnicity, religion nationality, time, place, or possessions-based but paradoxically it's universal only when one relinquishes the need to have an identity. The Satvik person can retrain his or her mind, turn it inward, and detach from the senses and yet be totally in the moment.

Satvik traits include minimalism, surrender and acceptance, the pursuit of contentment and self-realization, and living in the moment without any anticipation or expectation. Ignorance, capriciousness, laziness, or jealousy and attachments are viewed as obstructions. Quiet is preferred over talking, fasting is preferred over feasting, and stillness is preferred over hurrying.

An individual may not completely embody all the traits of any one personality type. It is more likely that some traits may overlap with another personality type or change during the socialization process.

- Happiness. The concept of Happiness in Vedic psychology is different from pleasure, sense-based fixation or simply being aroused/stimulated. Drives and habits fueled by desires result eventually in bondage and suffering, a condition that is exactly the opposite of contentment. The prerequisites for arriving at the state of happiness are an absence of ambivalence and duality via focus on the here and now, neutralizing anticipations and expectations. Nirvana is the ultimate happiness, and it means "freedom from it all i.e. attachments, operating out of likes and dislikes, or needing to belong to any "ism or religion". Everything else is the beginning of the never-ending cycle of either pleasure or pain.

- The Big Picture. Contradiction and paradoxes are accepted as being part of The Big Picture, which is perpetually evolving, unfolding, being born, and dying. Understanding this ebb and flow is emphasized over the compulsion to change situations. Accepting universal interconnectedness and oneness is emphasized over the need to isolate, separate, compete, or become attached to one's ego.

- Actions/Karma. Selfish karma, driven by ulterior motives, always leads to attachment and its negative consequences. Actions must be selfless, without attachment or anticipating or expecting anything.

The principles and practices of Vedic psychology offer an efficient, effective, and comprehensive psycho-somato-socio-spiritual approach for good mental hygiene and harmonious day-to-day living. It also provides the framework for genuine personality transformation either via total self-help or under the mentorship of a Guru. It is the same as psychotherapy; just the lingo is different as well as some procedures.

The Vedic and Sankhya yoga approach to mental hygiene views the individual as a whole i.e. mind-body-environment and spirituality. It does not infinitely divide human beings into minute particles, symptoms or traits. This is a very cost effective method and, as a result, often the problems of addictions, negative habits and lifestyle, low self-esteem, and interpersonal conflicts become insignificant, and symptoms often disappear spontaneously. Of course, these approaches are not applicable when someone is in a crisis such as intoxication, mental breakdown, episode or mania, or in the case of suicidal behavior.

INTEGRATION OF CROSS-CULTURAL PSYCHOLOGY

The world has become small and in many ways the West and East are rapidly merging and fusing in somewhat constructive ways. In the world of psychology and mental health, two developments have loosened the stranglehold of psychoanalytical and behaviorist approaches and shaped a Western openness to integrating the psychologies of the East. The 1960s and 1970s gave birth to the increasing popularity of meditation and Patanjali's Sankhya-Yoga in the West and a corresponding interest in the study of consciousness. At the same time, the emergence of transpersonal psychology also brought to focus the Indian psycho-spiritual and socio-philosophical traditions as valuable resources for understanding the nature of mind and consciousness. Western practitioners have integrated rather well many of the clinical procedures from Vedanta and Buddhism. Ignorantly, Buddhism is mistaken as separate and independent from Hinduism.

A parallel phenomenon occurred in India, as psychologists in the 1960s began to Indianize the prevailing Euro-American discipline and integrate their practice with Indian thought. This has given rise to the creation of an Indian psychology discipline that is rooted in traditional Indian philosophies and practices that have existed for at least the last 5000 years. A manifesto, signed by the delegates of a 2002 conference on Indian Psychology, outlines the intention of this approach, "Rich in content, sophisticated in its methods and valuable in its applied aspects, Indian psychology is pregnant with possibilities for the birth of new models in psychology that would have relevance not only for India but also for psychology in general."

Although this integration is underway, the mainstream of psychology involves a behavioral methodology that is incompatible with the needs of Indians. Although it is unrealistic to expect non-Indian therapists to adapt totally to the principles and practices of Vedic psychology, they will have more success with their Indian patients if they utilize some Vedic methods as an adjunct to their clinical approach such as mindfulness, breathing techniques, meditations, etc. These tools may be integrated in much the same way that Western relaxation techniques, imagery, biofeedback, pain management, hypnosis, and cognitive behavioral techniques are applied in the East.

Within this emerging integration, it is essential to incorporate somato-psycho-socio-spiritualistic principles that are at the core of Vedic psychotherapy. Cognitive, psychoanalytical, and behavioral-oriented therapies do not offer adequate solutions to the problems of an individual as a whole. On the contrary, therapeutic changes in the absence of philosophical and lifestyle changes often leave the individual in an adversarial frame of mind and promote alienation from society.

A truly cross-cultural psychology must expand its boundaries, taking the best from East and West. It must uphold human rights, be grounded in non-religious spirituality, be conducted with scientific rigor, and have at its core a commitment to serve humanity.

Psychology without human rights is but a practice of master manipulation of the weak by the strong, of the peace loving by the militant, and the domination of the laborer by the rich. It is a chaos where neither elderly, nor women, nor children are safe, and all privileges are for a selected and favored few.

Religion without spirituality promotes warfare and violence through Proselytization by self-proclaimed saviors who destroy indigenous cultures, their psychological identities and the very essence/soul of their culture that gives them meaning, purpose, and direction in life. Converts' names are changed, and they are asked to eat what has been taboo in their original culture just to speed up alienation and sever them from the roots of their origin and relatives. Divide and conquer still works.

Psychology without scientific rigor is nothing more than the practice of prejudices, stereotypes, and biases. Scientific rigor however, has to be open to integrate cross culture, and methodology limitations. Without the balance of intuition and reason, and the comparison of individual and collective therapeutic results, psychology will be little better than empathetic listening and relying on the innate skill of the practitioner.

Psychology without the commitment to serve mankind (spirituality) will be nothing but a fancy mental exercise, ivory tower head games and above all, a money-grabbing venture disguised as science. The poor, indigenous, have-nots, minorities, and underprivileged will be left out to rot in the prisons, confined in mental hospitals, or to beg for day to day survival.

In reality, cross-cultural psychology cannot be practiced if the psychology is not congruent with the indigenous culture while at the same time incorporating higher universal psycho-spiritual values and ideals. If psychology is to flourish, it will require an absolute commitment to finding a transparent, multidimensional, interdisciplinary, and universal humanitarian composite.

Individuals or individual societies emerge, evolve and prosper in the larger context of their unique history, geography, encounters with others, distinctive struggles for survival, and responses to unfamiliar threats. As the world has become a global village, it can be safely said that the evolution of the emerging practice of cross-cultural psychology will have a positive impact on our future progression and collective future. In order to be true scientists and effective practitioners, we need to realize that our individual cultures and backgrounds do not have all the answers; we all need to ask the relevant questions for the sake of those who are different from us. We need to expand our boundaries and become true world citizens. The Bhagavad Gita incorporated the concept very succinctly:

"The world is one family."

Appendix A: Hindu American Foundation Executive Summary

The advocacy group Hindu America Foundation (HAF) conducts surveys on the state of human rights in Asian diasporic countries, many of which in recent years have exhibited racist policies towards Indians.

What follows are capsule summaries of their report (2011).

PEOPLE'S REPUBLIC OF BANGLADESH

- In 1947, Hindus constituted nearly 30% of Bangladesh's population. By 1991, an estimated 20 million Hindus were "missing" from Bangladesh. Today, Hindus comprise less than 10% of the population.
- Bangladesh passed the Vested Properties Return (Amendment) Bill 2011, which enables Hindus to reclaim land and property confiscated by the government or looted and occupied by Muslims after the passage of the 1965 Vested Enemy Property Act (by Pakistan) and subsequently, the 1974 Vested Property Act. It is unclear, however, whether this Bill will be successfully implemented and enforced.
- Nearly 1.2 million, or 44%, of the 2.7 million Hindu households in the country were affected by the Enemy Property Act 1965 and its post-independence version, the Vested Property Act of 1974. Hindu-owned land continues to be illegally confiscated with the tacit or active support of government actors.
- Hindus from Bangladesh continue to be victims of ethnic cleansing waged by Islamic fundamentalists that include daily acts of murder, rape, kidnapping, forced conversions, temple destruction, and physical intimidation.

- Fifty-nine acts of murder, rape, kidnapping, temple destruction, and land encroachments targeting Hindus have been recorded in this report. The reduction in the number of attacks against Hindus after Sheikh Hasina assumed power three years ago, while encouraging, is still indicative of the oppressive conditions Hindus in Bangladesh live in. One expert estimates that there will be no Hindus left in Bangladesh in about 25 years.
- Human rights activists and journalists continue to be harassed and intimidated.
- Bangladesh has afforded new and extensive powers to their Human Rights Commission, but a Minorities Commission to monitor the specific human rights of minorities and to provide redress to minority grievances has yet to be established.
- The Hasina government set up a War Crimes Tribunal to prosecute those accused of the rape, murder, and genocide of ethnic Bengalis (mostly Hindus) during Bangladesh's struggle for independence in 1971.
- The commission inquiring into the attacks by the BNP (Bangladeshi Nationalist Party)--- Jamaat alliance against Hindus during the 2001 elections found that 26,352 people, including 25 ministers and lawmakers of the BNP- Jamaat alliance government, were involved in perpetrating the violence. The commission said there had been more than 18,000 incidents of major crimes, including murder, rape, arson, and looting by members of the then ruling BNP- Jamaat alliance in the 15 months following October 2001.

KINGDOM OF BHUTAN

- Bhutan is a multi-religious, multicultural, multiethnic, and multilingual society.
- Bhutan held its first National Assembly elections in 2008, transitioning to a democratic constitutional monarchy.
- Bhutan presented its first human rights report to the Universal Periodic Report Review Committee of the UN Human Rights

Council in Geneva on December 4, 2009. It sought to present itself as a guarantor of human rights. Bhutan's marginalized minorities, however, protested against the government's human rights record in Geneva.

- Bhutan received 99 recommendations from the Human Rights Council when it presented its report on the human rights situation in the country. The government accepted a majority of the recommendations.

- Bhutan evicted over 100,000 Hindu minority and Nyingmapa Buddhists from Southern and Eastern Bhutan in the early 1990s.

- More than 100,000 Bhutanese citizens, nearly one-sixth of the kingdom's total population of approximately 700,000, have been forced to leave or have been forcibly evicted from the country by the royal regime solely on the basis of their religious/ethnic identity.

- Over 100,000 Bhutanese refugees are living in refugee camps in Nepal managed by the United Nations High Commission for Refugees (UNHCR), while another 20,000 undocumented refugees are scattered outside the camps in Nepal and several Indian states without any help or legal status. The United States agreed to accept 60,000 Hindu refugees, with the first group arriving in 2008.

- More than 43,500 Bhutanese refugees have been resettled, including more than 37,000 in the United States.

REPUBLIC OF THE FIJI ISLANDS

- In Fiji, Hindus constitute approximately 34% of the Christian majority state.

- Fijian Hindus faced hate speech, and Hindu temples were targets of attack until 2008. Such attacks appeared to have ceased in 2009. In 2011, Hindus continued to enjoy a respite from religious/criminal attacks.

- The Methodist Church of Fiji has repeatedly called for the creation of a Christian State.

- It is encouraging that the interim government of Prime Minister Bainarmirama has committed itself to the protection of minorities, especially the large Hindu minority.
- The Bainarmirama regime has been accused of violating the fundamental rights of its citizens and suppressing political dissent.

INDIAN STATE OF JAMMU AND KASHMIR

- The Maharaja of Kashmir legally ceded his kingdom to India in 1947 when Pakistan invaded Kashmir in order to conquer the kingdom. Pakistan occupies about 35% of the region, India governs approximately half, and China occupies the remainder of the region, including a portion ceded to it by Pakistan.
- India and Pakistan have fought major wars over Kashmir.
- Since the mid to late 1980s, Islamist terrorists, supported and trained by Pakistan, have targeted Kashmir and are guilty of the large scale ethnic cleansing of Hindus from India's Kashmir Valley.
- More than 300,000 Kashmiri Hindus are refugees in their own country, sheltered in temporary camps in Jammu and other parts of India.
- 2011 did not see any significant resolution to the plight of Hindu refugees from Kashmir. The few attempts to redress the situation by the Central and State Governments seem desultory in nature, and Kashmiri Pundits continue to live in abject conditions in "refugee camps."

MALAYSIA

- Malaysia is a self-declared Islamic Republic, and Islam is the official religion of the country, despite it being a multiethnic and multi-religious country in which Hindus, Christians, and Buddhists are significant minorities. Minorities struggle to maintain and practice their religions. The right to religious freedom has been progressively deteriorating in recent years. Ethnic Malays are required to be Muslims, as they are born into Islam and do not have the freedom to convert.

- The Hindu population faces discrimination and intimidation, including the destruction of its temples and places of worship. The government continues to treat pre-independence era Hindu temples differently than mosques from the same era and gives preference to mosques in the allocation of public funds and lands.
- Hindu activists and leaders have been systematically persecuted by government officials, and public dissent has been brutally repressed through the use of draconian internal security laws. There have been several recent cases forcing Hindus and other minorities to deal with the Islamic Sharia courts where they face severe disadvantages.

ISLAMIC REPUBLIC OF PAKISTAN

- In 1947, Hindus were approximately 25% of the population of Pakistan. Now, Hindus constitute less than 1.6% of the population.
- Pakistan officially and routinely discriminates against non-Muslims through a variety of discriminatory laws, such as blasphemy laws.
- On March 24, 2005, Pakistan restored the discriminatory practice of mandating the inclusion of the religious identity of individuals in all new passports.
- School textbooks continue to promote Islam and hatred and intolerance towards non-Muslims, particularly Hindus. Islamists continue to extend their influence throughout the Federally Administered Tribal Areas (FATA), and other parts of Khyber Pakhtunkhwa Province, where they are increasingly enforcing Islamic law.
- Recurring reports point to an alarming trend of Hindu girls being kidnapped, raped, held in *madrassas* (Islamic

seminaries), and forcibly converted to Islam.

- Poor Hindus continue to be subjected to inhumane conditions through the bonded labor system.

DEMOCRATIC SOCIALIST REPUBLIC OF SRI LANKA

- Sri Lanka is a multi-ethnic, multi-religious nation that was plagued by years of ethnic conflict. The violent conflict between the Sinhala, majority Sri Lankan government, and the Tamil groups was the result of a combination of religious, ethnic, and linguistic factors. Tensions between the Sinhalese majority and Tamil separatists in northern Sri Lanka erupted into war in 1983. The civil war came to an end in May 2009.
- Not all Tamils are Hindus and the LTTE, the primary Tamil terrorist outfit, was not a Hindu organization.
- The prolonged conflict was detrimental to all Sri Lankans, especially the large Hindu minority population, which experienced an undue share of violence and displacement.
- The plight of innocent civilians continued to deteriorate as fighting between government forces and the Tamil Tigers intensified and came to a bitter end in 2009. Both sides are guilty of severe human rights violations and war crimes.

REPUBLIC OF TRINIDAD AND TOBAGO

- The country is a multi-ethnic, multi-religious island nation with Hindu Indo-Trinidadians and Afro-Trinidadians accounting for the majority of the population. Roman Catholics and Hindus make up the largest religious groups.
- The racial and religious animosity between Afro-Caribbean and Indo-Caribbeans has been exacerbated over the years. Hindus are frequently subjected to discrimination, hate speech, and acts of violence.
- Indo-Trinidadians have been systematically denied government benefits and employment in public sector jobs.

Hindu institutions and festivals are subject to acts of violence and are denied equal access to public funds.

- A new government, headed by Kamla Persad Bissessar of Indian descent, took office in May 2010. It is expected that nearly six decades of discrimination against Indo-Caribbeans will come to an end.

Appendix B: HAF Country Specific Recommendations

What follows are the Hindu American Foundation's country specific recommendations for those its report (2011), *Hindus in South Asia and the Diaspora: A Survey of Human Rights*

PEOPLE'S REPUBLIC OF BANGLADESH

- The Awami League government, led by Sheikh Hasina, must continue to take substantial and verifiable measures to ensure that attacks on Hindus and their institutions cease and bring to swift justice those political and radical religious elements that have led the assault on Hindus and other minorities.
- Bangladesh must take all necessary actions to effectively implement the Vested Properties Return (Amendment) Bill 2011 and ensure that confiscated lands are returned to the rightful, original owners.
- Bangladesh must set up a Minorities Commission to redress minority grievances and repair systemic and structural deficiencies that have made minorities second-class citizens in the country.
- The USA and other donor nations must demand accountability from the Bangladesh Government, and all aid to Bangladesh should be contingent on the improvement of the human rights situation.

KINGDOM OF BHUTAN

- Bhutan must take concrete steps to demonstrate its stated commitment to a just resolution of the longstanding refugee crisis.
- Bhutan, Nepal, and the UNHCR should adopt a Memorandum

of Understanding (MOU) for voluntary repatriation that includes a clear statement of rights and entitlements upon the refugees' return to Bhutan—including full citizenship rights and human rights protections.

- Donors, UN agencies, and Bhutan's other partners should insist on measures to eliminate discrimination against the Hindu Lhotshampas and ensure the protection of their fundamental human rights and their rights to participate as full citizens of Bhutan.

REPUBLIC OF THE FIJI ISLANDS

- The Fijian government must respect the rights of all citizens, and the inherent political bias against ethnic Indians must be eradicated.
- Fiji should repeal the "Truth and Reconciliation" (TRC) Bill and successfully prosecute and punish the criminals of the 2000 coup.
- Fiji must continue to be vigilant in the protection of Hindus from violence and hate speech, and it must institute permanent safeguards to protect Hindu temples from attacks.
- The Fijian government must distance itself from Christian fundamentalists promoting hatred against Hindus and Hinduism and avoid Christianization of its institutions.

INDIAN STATE OF JAMMU AND KASHMIR

- Kashmiri Hindus must be allowed to return to their homes, have their property restored to them, and receive protection from the Indian government and the Kashmir State Government.
- The State Government must end the economic and political marginalization of Hindus and Buddhists in the state and provide full protection and accommodation to Hindu pilgrims and pilgrimage sites.

- Pakistan must permanently end its sponsorship of terror via direct military aid to terror groups, sponsorship of terror camps in Pakistan, and covert support to terrorists by its Inter-Services Intelligence (ISI) spy service.
- U.S. policy makers and Congressional Representatives must exert pressure on Pakistan to end its use of terrorism as an instrument of state policy and should support H. Res. 387 to send a strong message in support of the Kashmiri Pandits.

MALAYSIA

- Religious freedom should be allowed and encouraged for ethnic Malays and the minority religious populations in the country.
- Religious minorities should not be forced to deal with the country's Islamic Sharia courts.
- The United States, United Nations, the international community, and human rights groups should pressure the Malaysian government to protect Hindu temples from desecration and destruction. Hindu places of worship that existed prior to independence should be designated as temple property, and the title to the land should be handed to the respective temple trustees and committees as has been done for pre- independence era mosques.
- The Malaysian Government should be urged to not discriminate in the allocation of public funds and land for places of worship between Muslim and minority religious groups.
- The U.S. should revisit its trade ties with Malaysia and restrict any future appropriations unless the government protects the human rights of its ethnic and religious minorities, repeals the repressive Internal Security Act (ISA), and ends its affirmative action policies favoring the majority Muslim Malays (*bumiputras*).

ISLAMIC REPUBLIC OF PAKISTAN

- The Government of Pakistan must take immediate steps for the protection of Hindus from rape, kidnapping, and forced conversions.
- Religious minorities must be allowed to independently manage their religious institutions free from government interference, and representatives from the Hindu and Sikh communities should be given full control over the Evacuee Trust Property Board (ETPB).
- Pakistan should reform its education system to remove inaccuracies about other religions and promote tolerance and pluralism.
- The United States should demand that Pakistan stop all support and financing of Islamic militant groups operating in the subcontinent. The USA must place strict conditions on any financial assistance to Pakistan and demand accountability for human rights violations.
- Pakistan should establish a truly independent Human Rights Commission and a National Minorities Commission to monitor the human rights conditions and to enable minorities to enjoy the rights provided to the majority population.

DEMOCRATIC SOCIALIST REPUBLIC OF SRI LANKA

- HAF expresses grave concern that the Hindu institutions and Tamil culture in Sri Lanka were severely threatened over the past few decades, and this threat was exacerbated by the civil war. The government should hasten to protect Hindu institutions from harm.
- The government must quickly release the remaining Tamil civilians still held in refugee camps and provide all of the support in the rehabilitation and resettlement of the displaced Tamil population.

- President Rajapaksa, reelected to a five-year term in January 2010, should set up a war crimes tribunal, allow international journalists freedom to report from Sri Lanka, and begin serious talks with Tamil leaders and other minority groups to create an equitable political and social dispensation in the country.

REPUBLIC OF TRINIDAD AND TOBAGO

- The United States should encourage the current Trinidad government to abide by the country's constitution and guarantee safety and security to Hindus and Indo-Trinidadians.
- The Trinidadian government should practice parity and equality in government response to and support of various ethnic and religious groups. Trinidad must do more to protect Hindus from violence, hate speech, and racial and religious stereotyping. Furthermore, the government must safeguard Hindu temples from attacks.
- The Trinidadian government must prosecute Christian fundamentalists who promote hatred against Hindus and Hinduism.

Appendix C: List of Mental Disorders

The following list has been adapted from the ICD9, DSM IV-TR, and other sources.

Disorders first diagnosed by age 18

- Mental Retardation; Mild, Moderate, Severe, Profound or Unspecified
- Learning Disorders; Reading, Mathematics, Written Expression or Nonspecific
- Communication Disorders; Expressive Language, Mixed Receptive-Expressive, Phonological, Stuttering or Communication Disorder NOS
- Pervasive Developmental Disorder; Autistic, Rett's, Childhood Disintegrative, Asperger's or Pervasive Developmental Disorder NOS
- Attention Deficit & Disruptive Disorders; Attention-Deficit/Hyperactivity Disorder, Combined Type, Predominantly Inattentive Type, Predominantly Hyperactive-Impulsive Type, Attention Deficit/Hyperactivity Disorder NOS, Conduct Disorder, Oppositional Defiant Disorder or Disruptive Behavior Disorder
- Feeding & Eating Disorder of Infancy/Early Childhood; Pica, Rumination Disorder, or Feeding Disorder
- Tic Disorders; Tourette's, Chronic Motor or Vocal Tic, Transient Tic or Tic Disorder
- Eliminations Disorder; Encopresis, With constipation & Overflow, Without Constipation & Overflow or Enuresis (Non-Medical caused)
- Other Disorders of Infancy/Childhood/Adolescence; Separation Anxiety, Selective Mutism, Reactive Attachment, Stereotypic Movement or Not Otherwise Specified/NOS
- Delirium; Due to General Medical Condition, Substance Intoxication, Substance Withdrawal, Multiple Etiology,

Delirium NOS Amnestic Disorders;

- Due to General Medical Condition/Substance-Induced Persisting or NOS
- Dementia; Alzheimer's Type (Uncomplicated/With Delusions/With Depressed Mood)
- Vascular Dementia; (Uncomplicated/With Delusions/With Depressed Mood)
- Dementia Due to Creutzfeldt-Jacob Disease
- Dementia Due to HIV Disease
- Dementia Due to Head Trauma
- Dementia Due to Huntington's Disease
- Dementia Due to Medical Condition
- Dementia Due to Multiple Etiologies or NOS
- Dementia Due to Parkinson's Disease
- Dementia Due to Pick's Disease
- Substance-Induced Persisting Dementia
- Other Cognitive Disorders
- Mental Disorders Due to a General Medical Condition; Catatonic, Personality Change Due to Medical Condition
- Substance-Related Disorders (Bhang, Tadee, Beer, Wine, Hard Liquor); Dependence on Alcohol or Abuse of Alcohol, Alcohol Withdrawal/Alcohol Intoxication Delirium/Alcohol Withdrawal Delirium/Alcohol-Induced Persisting Amnesic Disorder/Alcohol-Induced Psychotic Disorder (With Delusions/With Hallucinations, Alcohol-Induced Mood Disorder/Alcohol-Induced Anxiety Disorder/Alcohol-Induced Sexual Dysfunction/ Alcohol-Induced Sleep Disorder
- Amphetamine or Similar Drug Related Disorder (Speed, Uppers, Crank, Black Beauties, Crystal; Amphetamine Dependence/Abuse/Intoxication/Intoxication With Perceptual Disturbances/Withdrawal/Intoxication Delirium/Induced Psychotic Disorder (with Delusions/With hallucinations)/Induced Mood Disorder/Induced Anxiety Disorder/Induced Sexual Dysfunction / Induced Sleep Disorder/NOS

- Caffeine-Induced Disorders; Intoxication/Induced Anxiety Disorder/Induced Sleep Disorder or NOS
- Cannabis (dope, pot, grass, weed, herb, hash, joint) Related Disorders; Dependence/Abuse, Intoxication/ Intoxication With Perceptual Disturbances/Intoxication Delirium/Induced Psychotic Disorder (With Delusions/With Hallucinations), Induced Anxiety Disorder or NOS
- Cocaine Use Disorders (Coke, Rock, Crack, Base); Intoxication/Intoxication With Perceptual Disturbances, Withdrawal, Intoxication Delirium, Induced Psychotic Disorder I with delusions/With Hallucinations)/Induced mood disorder/Induced Anxiety Disorder/Induced Sexual Dysfunction/Induced Sleep Disorder or Induced Related NOS
- Hallucinogen Related Disorder; Dependence/Abuse, Persisting Perceptual Disorder/NOS
- Inhalant Related Disorders (gas, aerosols, glue, nitrites, rush, whiteout); Dependence/Abuse, Intoxication/Intoxication /Intoxication/Intoxication Delirium, Induced Persisting Dementia/Induced Psychotic Disorder (With Delusions/With Hallucinations)/Induced Mood Disorder/Induced Anxiety Disorder or NOS
- Nicotine Related Disorder; Dependence, Withdrawal or NOS
- Opioid Use Disorders (Heroin, Morphine, Codeine, Dilaudid, Demerol, Black Tar, China White); Dependence/Abuse, Intoxication, Intoxication with Perceptual Disturbances, Withdrawal, Intoxication Delirium, Induced Psychotic Disorder (With Delusions/With Hallucinations), Induced Mood Disorder. Induced Sexual Dysfunction, Induced Sleep Disorder or NOS
- Phencyclidine/Like Related Disorder; Dependence/abuse, Intoxication, Intoxication With Perceptual Disturbances, Intoxication Delirium, Induced Psychotic Disorder (With Delusions/With hallucinations), Induced Mood Disorder, Induced Anxiety Disorder or NOS

- Sedative, Hypnotic, Or Anxiolytic Related Disorder (Kava Kava, Barbiturates, downers, tranquilizers, ludes, reds, Valium, Xanax; Dependence/Abuse, Intoxication, Withdrawal, Intoxication Delirium, Induced Persisting Dementia, Induced Persisting Amnestic Disorder, Induced Psychotic Disorder (With Delusions/With Hallucinations), Induced Mood Disorder/Induced Anxiety Disorder, Induced Sexual Dysfunction, Induced Sleep Disorder or NOS
- Poly-substance i.e. simultaneous use of many drugs abuse Related Disorder
- Other drugs or substance of unknown names or origin such as Dhatura.
- Psychotic Disorders such as Schizophrenia; Paranoid Type, Disorganized Type, Catatonic Type, Undifferentiated Type, or Residual Type
- Schizophreniform Disorder
- Schizoaffective Disorder (psychosis + mood disorder combined); Bipolar Type, Depressive Type
- Delusional Disorder (cognitive distortions)
- Brief Psychotic Disorder (With or Without Marked Stressor)
- Shared Psychotic Disorder
- Psychotic Disorder Due to General Medical Condition (With Delusions &/or With Hallucinations)
- Substance (alcohol or drugs, prescribed or illegal) Induced Psychotic Disorders
- Psychotic Disorder NOS
- Mood Disorders
- Major Depression (Single Episode/Recurrent)
- Dysthymic Disorder (garden variety depression due to loss or disappointments)
- Depressive Disorder NOS
- Bipolar/Manic Depressive Disorders
- Bipolar I (Single Manic Episode/Mixed, Most Recent Episode Hypomanic/ Most Recent Episode Manic/Most Recent Episode Mixed/Most Recent Episode Depressed/Most Recent

Episode Unspecified
- Bipolar Disorder II
- Cyclothymic Disorder
- Bipolar Disorder NOS
- Mood Disorder Due to General Medical Condition. (With Depressive Features/ With Major Depression Episode/With Manic Features/With Mixed Features)
- Substance-Induced Mood Disorder
- Mood Disorder NOS
- Anxiety Disorders (Panic & with or Without Agoraphobia)
- Agoraphobia with or without History of Panic Disorder
- Specific Phobias (Animal Type/Natural Environment Type/Blood-Injection-Injury Type/Situational Type/Other Type)
- Social Phobia
- Obsessive-Compulsive Disorder (OCD)
- Post-traumatic stress disorder/PTSD (Acute/Chronic/ With Delayed Onset)
- Acute Stress Disorder
- Generalized Anxiety Disorder (GAD/Worrying/chinta)
- Anxiety Due to Generalized Medical Condition (With Panic Attacks/With Obsessive-Compulsive Symptoms)
- Substance-Induced Anxiety Disorder
- Anxiety Disorder NOS
- Somatoform Disorder (Somatization/Undifferentiated. Somatoform/Conversion With Motor Symptom/Or Deficit/With Seizures or Convulsions/With Sensory Symptom/Deficit/With Mixed Presentation)
- Pain Disorder (Associated With Psychological Factors/Both With Psychological Factors & a General Medical Condition)
- Hypochondriasis (With Poor Insight)
- Body Dysmorphic Disorder
- Somatoform Disorder NOS

- Factitious Disorders (With Predominantly Psychological Signs& Symptoms/Physical Signs & Symptoms/combined Signs & Symptoms or NOS)
- Dissociative Disorders (Dissociative Amnesia/Fugue)
- Dissociative Identity Disorder
- Depersonalization Disorder
- Dissociative Disorder NOS
- Sexual & Gender Identity Disorder
- Sexual Dysfunctions; Lifelong Type/Acquired Type/Generalized Type/Situational Type/Due to Psychological Factors/Combined Factors)
- Sexual Desire Disorders; Hypoactive/Aversion
- Sexual Arousal Disorders; (Female Arousal/Male Erectile Disorder (ED))
- Orgasmic Disorders; Female Orgasmic/Male Orgasmic/Premature Sexual Pain Disorders; Dyspareunia /Vaginusmus (Not Due to General Medical Condition)
- Sexual Dysfunction Due to a General Medical Condition; Female Hypoactive Sexual Desire/Male Hypoactive Sexual Desire/Male Erectile Disorder/Female Dyspareunia/Male Dyspareunia/ Other Female Sexual Dysfunction/ Other Male Sexual Dysfunction/Substance-Induced Sexual Dysfunction
- Paraphilias; Exhibitionism/Fetishism/Frotteurism/Pedophilia (Attracted to Male/to Female/to both/Limited to Incest/)/Sexual Masochism/Sadism/Transvestic Fetishism/Voyeurism/Paraphilia NOS
- Gender Identity Disorder; NOS
- Sexual Disorder NOS
- Eating Disorders; Anorexia Nervosa/Bulimia Nervosa/NOS
- Sleep Disorders
- Dyssomnias (Primary Insomnia/ Primary Hypersomnia/ Narcolepsy/ Breathing Related Sleep Disorder/ Circadian Rhythm Sleep Disorder/ NOS0
- Parasomnias; Nightmare Disorder/Sleep Terror Disorder/ Sleep-walking Disorder/ NOS

- Sleep Disorders Related to Another Mental Disorder
- Sleep Disorders Due to General Medical Condition
- Substance-Induced Sleep Disorder
- Impulse-Control Disorders; Intermittent Explosive Disorder/ Kleptomania/ Pathological Gambling/ Trichotillmania/ Impulse Control Disorder NOS
- Adjustment Disorders; With Depressed Mood/With Anxiety/Both/With Disturbance of Conduct/Mixed Disturbance of Emotions and Conduct/Unspecified
- Personality Disorders; Paranoid Personality /Schizoid/ Schizotypal/ Antisocial /Borderline/ Histrionic/ Narcissistic/Avoidant /Dependent/ Obsessive-Compulsive/ NOS
- Psychological Factors Affecting Medical Condition; Mental disorder affecting Medical Condition/Psychological Symptoms Affecting Medical Condition/Personality Traits Or Coping Style Affecting Medical Condition/Maladaptive Health Behaviors Affecting Medical Condition/Stress related Physiological Response Affecting Medical Condition/Other or Unspecified Psychological Factors Affecting Medical Condition
- Medication Induced Movement Disorder; Neuroleptic Induced Parkinsonianism/Malignant Syndrome/Acute Dystonia/Tardive Dyskinesia/Postural Tremor/NOS Movement Disorder
- Adverse Effects of Medication NOS
- Relational Problems; Related to a Mental Disorder or General Medical Condition/Parent Child problem/ Partner Problem/ Sibling Problem/ Relational Problem NOS
- Problems Related to Abuse or Neglect; Physical Abuse of Child/Sexual Abuse of Child/Neglect of Child/Physical Abuse of Adult/Sexual Abuse of Adult
- Additional Conditions That May be a Focus of Clinical Attention

- Noncompliance with Treatment
- Malingering
- Child or Adolescent Antisocial Behavior
- Borderline Intellectual Functioning (IQ 70-90)
- Age Relative Cognitive Decline
- Bereavement
- Academic Problem
- Occupational Problem
- Identity Problem
- Religious or Spiritual Problem
- Acculturation Problem
- Phase of Life Problem
- List of Other problem Behaviors that need mention
- Pyromania-Fire setting Behavior
- Erotomania-Sexual fixation on specific person
- Cultural (Cross) Shock and Adjustment Difficulties
- Religious Fanaticism-Believing that people of other faith should be killed, converted, made to suffer, etc.
- Pathological Nationalism-Belief that other nationalities. ethnic groups are inferior, undeserving
- Chauvinism-Believing that people of other genders are inferior and should be socio-Politically/economically deprived.

NEUROLOGICAL PROBLEMS

Neurological problems present a very difficult challenge because they are difficult to diagnose, mimic many other diseases, and treatment options are rather limited. Unfortunately, many Primary Care Physicians, specialists, and schools do not fully utilize neurological consultations. Ideally, your PCP, psychologist, and school nurse should be able to understand when a neurologist consultation is indicated.

The following is a brief list of some neurological disorders. Provided they are not due to substance abuse, typical symptoms include confusion, disorientation, speech impairment, high distractibility, agitation and hyper-stimulation, inappropriate verbalizations, difficulty with memory and recall, no response to touch, sound, pain or sight, inconsistent response to commands, aggressive, bizarre, non-purposeful behavior, and short attention span.

- Frontal Lobe Dysfunctions/damage/epilepsy
- Epilepsy
- Cerebrovascular Accident (stroke)
- Aphasia, memory deficits, intoxication, attention disorders also have neurology correlates.
- Toxicity (metals, chemicals, overdose, etc.)

Problems of very young children

- Childhood depression
- Encopresis
- Enuresis
- Bed-wetting
- Temper Tantrums
- Acting out around meal time
- Acting out while socializing or in the shopping malls.
- Restlessness while confined in the car for long distance driving
- Excessive fears/shyness, avoidance
- Problem behavior around bedtime/sleep
- Toilet training/constipation
- Fetal Alcohol Syndrome
- Mutism/selective Mutism

SUMMARY

- Mental health issues are only indicative of us and our humanity. None of us is above being vulnerable or totally immune to feeling our feelings, thinking our thoughts, or ending up behaving in ways that are contrary to our belief system or the society's expectations. Individual and society have always been engaged in a perpetual dance of seeking independence and freedom while society is enforcing conformity and surrender.

- Religions of the word are the old psychologies emerged to help and manage individuals and social issues. The reason they have become obsolete in our era is only because they have a rigid belief that if one is good one will be happy. The reality of being human is more complex, and goodness does not guarantee happiness nor vice versa. Religions will continue to fail and become less effective with human beings because of their excessive dependence on fear, guilt, and hierarchy as controlling tools. Modern men and women are seeking autonomy and yet spirituality free from religion.

- Modern psychology's biggest contribution has been to point out that feelings are real, powerful, and cannot be always suppressed or repressed. Hindu psychology's major contribution has been to offer highly sophisticated procedures to promote sublimation as a tool to manage feelings but also to integrate the complex reality of feelings and psycho-socio-econo-spiritual demands via the four ashramas: Brahmacharya, Grihastha, Vanaprastha, and Sanyasa. Psychology will remain the new religion of the mankind and prove more efficient once it further merges and integrates East and West, North and South.

- Mental health professionals have a calling, beyond being entrepreneurs and specialists. Society needs mental health services from private practice to outpatient care to mental health institutions. The world is vast, and no needy individual can be left behind. The issue is not to always achieve success but to ensure every person access, to be mindful of diversity, and to maintain transparency. Mental health services cannot operate by being devoid of spirituality. The social worker and the psychiatrist must bridge the gap between their professions.

- Each patient comes with a background of not only

individuality but of religion, culture, family traditions, and the geopolitical context of his development. Mental health professionals and service providers will be ill-equipped if they are not culturally sensitive. For optimum results, each country, culture, religion, and ethnic society needs to train mental service providers to meet their specific needs. The Indian Diaspora is huge, scattered the world over, and is overdue for mental health services. The stress and the strains of living in alien cultures and socio-economic-political and religious threats have depleted the Diaspora. Religion has provided the basic strength but the resilience is thinning and the hope receding. Indians, like the Vanaprastha Corps, Doctors without Borders, and many other volunteer groups have to start organizing, sharing resources, and reaching out to places and people who have yet to learn what a mental health professional is. Education and information dissemination is the primary call. It should be followed by diagnostic assessments, proper referrals and ensuring positive outcomes. The international Indian community can adopt these causes as part of their Bhakti yoga and share resources to the communities in the Diaspora. Different temples and community organizations can assume responsibilities for specific projects i.e. domestic violence, Indians in foreign prisons, hotlines for crisis management, addiction counseling, and so on.

References

American Psychiatric Association. (2000). Diagnostic and statistical manual of mental disorders (4th ed., text rev.). Washington, DC: Author.

Baumann, M., Luchesi, B., & Wilke, A. (2003). Tempel und Tamilen in zweiter Heimat: Hindus aus Sri Lanka im deutschsprachigen und skandinavischen Raum. Würzburg: Ergon.

Bates, Crispin, editor. (2009) *Community, Empire and Migration: South Asians in the Diaspora*, New York: Palgrave.

Bean, R. A. and Titus, G. (2009), Cultural Intersection of Asian Indian Ethnicity and Presenting Problem: Adapting Multicultural Competence for Clinical Accessibility. Jnl Multicult Counseling & Dev, 37: 40–51. doi: 10.1002/j.2161-1912.2009.tb00090.x

Bhatia, S. (2007). American Karma: Race, Culture, and Identity in the Indian Diaspora. New York: NYU Press. Retrieved August 12, 2013, from Project MUSE database.

Bhattacharya, G. (1998). Drug Use among Asian-Indian adolescents: identifying protective/risk factors. Adolescence, 33(129), 169-184.

Bhattacharya, G. (2002). Drug abuse risks for acculturating immigrant adolescents: Case study of Asian Indians in the United States. Health & Social Work, 27(3), 175-183.

Caplan, L. (2001). Children of colonialism: Anglo-Indians in a postcolonial world. Oxford; New York: Berg.

Coward, H. G., Hinnells, J. R., & Williams, R. B. (2000). The South Asian religious diaspora in Britain, Canada, and the United States. Albany, N.Y.: State University of New York Press.

Dasgupta, S. D. (2007). Body evidence: Intimate violence against South Asian women in America. New Brunswick, N.J.; London: Rutgers University Press.

Desjarlais, R., Eisenberg, L., Good, B., & Kleinman, A. (1995). World Mental Health. New York, NY: Oxford Press. [Well-researched exposition on the major challenges in global mental health]

Dhingra, P. (2007). Managing multicultural lives: Asian American professionals and the challenge of multiple identities. Stanford, Calif: Stanford University Press.

House, A. E. (1999). DSM-IV diagnosis in the schools. New York: Guilford Press.

Mahabir, Noor Kumar, *East Indian Women of Trinidad and Tobago: An Annotated Bibliography,* Chakra Pub. House, 1992
This is the first book in the Caribbean that provides information on 236 successful Indian women. 130 carefully chosen photographs, some of which are in color, accompany the 218 annotated references.

Mahabir, Noor Kumar, *The Still Cry: Personal Accounts of East Indians in Trinidad and Tobago during Indentureship* (1845-1917), Calaloux Publications, 1985.
The reports of five surviving ex-indentured immigrant laborers are recorded verbatim to read like an epic poem. A woman, a Madras emigrant, a Muslim, a Brahmin, and a cocoa/rubber estate worker narrate the conditions of life in

village India when they left, the trauma of crossing the Kala Pani (Black Water), and the experience of adjusting to a new life among strangers under a driver and overseer on the sugarcane plantations of the New World.

Portman, T. A. A. (2001). Sex role attributions of American-Indian women. Journal of Mental Health Counseling, 23(1), 72-84. Chicago

Puwar, N., & Raghuram, P. (Eds.). (2003). South Asian women in the diaspora. Berg.

Safran, W. (2005). The Jewish diaspora in a comparative and theoretical perspective. Israel studies, 10(1), 36-60.

Singh, D. H., & Maharaj, R. (2006). Doon Pandit: His life and times (1900-1958). Chaguanas, Trinidad: Indian Review Press.
        This is a biography of the legendary Doon Pandit (1900-1958) who was a Hindu priest, community leader, and spiritual healer in colonial Trinidad. His reputation as a healer had spread from India to England, Venezuela, and other Caribbean islands. Perhaps his most recognized act was in curing Josephine Shaw, wife of the then-Governor of Trinidad. For the performance of this miracle, he was bestowed the honor of being named a Member of the British Empire (MBE) in 1949.

Sookdeo, N. A. (2000). Freedom, festivals and caste in Trinidad after slavery: a society in transition. Neil Sook-Deo.
        This book is about slavery, free labor, and racism. The chapters include information about the journey aboard the "coolie" ships from India, Trinidad in the nineteenth century, immigration and the demands of the plantation economy, education in the colony, colonial elites, Carnival, and the 1884 Hosay/Muharram riots.

Snyder, P. J., Nussbaum, P. D., & Robins, D. L. (2006). Clinical neuropsychology: A pocket handbook for assessment. American Psychological Association.

Sundberg, N. D., Rohila, P. K., & Tyler, L. E. (1970). Values of Indian and American adolescents. Journal of Personality and Social Psychology, 16(3), 374.

Warren, M. (2001). Behavioral Management Guide: Essential Treatment Strategies for Adult Psychotherapy. Jason Aronson.

The Hindu American Foundation is a non-profit 501(c)(3), non-partisan organization, promoting the Hindu and American ideals of understanding, tolerance, and pluralism.

Jacobsen, K. A. (2004). South Asians in the diaspora: histories and religious traditions/edited by Knut A. Jacobsen and P. Pratap Kumar. Brill.

Vertovec, S., & Vertovec, S. (2000). The Hindu diaspora: comparative patterns. London: Routledge.

Raleigh, V. S., Bulusu, L., & Balarajan, R. (1990). Suicides among immigrants from the Indian subcontinent. The British Journal of Psychiatry, 156(1), 46-50.

Rukmani, T. S. (1999). Hindu diaspora: Global perspectives. Chair in Hindu Studies, Dept. of Religion, Concordia University.

Williams, R. B. (Ed.). (1996). A Sacred Thread: Modern Transmission of Hindu Traditions in India and Abroad. Columbia University Press.

Vertovec, S. (1991). Aspects of the South Asian diaspora/edited by Steven Vertovec. Oxford University Press.

Witkin, H. A., & Berry, J. W. (1975). Psychological differentiation in cross-cultural perspective. Journal of cross-cultural psychology.

Additional Article Refere
Saran, P. (1980). Patterns of Adaptation of Indian Immigrants: Challenges and Strategies. In Uprooting and Development (pp. 375-399). Springer US.

Hodge, D. R. (2004). Working with Hindu clients in a spiritually sensitive manner. Social Work, 49(1), 27-38.

Desjarlais, R., Eisenberg, L., Good, B., and Kleinman, A. (1995). World mental health: Problems and priorities in low-income countries. Oxford University Press.

Lindner, E. G. (2002). Humiliation or dignity: Regional conflicts in the global village. Expediente, 146.

Varma, P. K. (2010). Becoming Indian. Penguin Books India.

Web References

Global Hindu Diaspora - A bibliography of books and main articles:
Http: //www.unilu.ch/files/bib-global-hindu-Diaspora.pdf

Mental Health Research in India
http://www.icmr.nic.in/publ/Mental%20Helth%20.Pdf

Pravasi Bharatiya Divas – Engaging the Diaspora:
The Way Forward
Http: //moia.gov.in/writereaddata/pdf/proceedings_2010.Pdf

An Ode to the Indian Diaspora – Little India
Http: //www.littleindia.com/nri/1388-an-ode-to-the-indian-Diaspora.Html

How India became America
Http: //www.nytimes.com/2012/03/11/opinion/sunday/how-india-became-america.html?Pagewanted=all

Story of Trishanku
Http: //en.wikipedia.org/wiki/Trishanku

Hindu American Foundation – Human Rights Reports
Http: //www.hafsite.org/resources/human_rights_report

India among countries with highest number of HIV adolescents
http://www.Deccanchronicle.com/channels/nation/north/india-among-countries-highest-number-hiv-adolescents-919

15 Commit Suicide every hour in India
http://www.Indiatribune.com/index.Php?option=com_content&view=article&id=7286:15-commit-suicide-every-hour-in-india-majority-victims-married-report&catid=125:general-news&Itemid=400

5,484 Kids raped, 1408 killed in 2010 in India.
http://articles.Timesofindia.Indiatimes.com/2011-10-30/india/30338511_1_cases-of-sexual-assault-uttar-pradesh-madhya-pradesh

Psychiatric training and therapies in Ayurveda
Http: //psycnet.apa.org/psycinfo/1986-18361-001

Personality types in Ayurveda.
Http: //psycnet.apa.org/psycinfo/1984-31446-001

Extension of mental health service through psychiatric camps: a
new approach
Http: //repository.ias.ac.in/31108/

Indian Thought and Tradition: a Psycho-historical perspective.
Http: //ipi.org.in/texts/kirankumar/kk-ip-history.php

ISSN 1393-614X Minerva - An Internet Journal of Philosophy
Vol. 9 2005. Freud's Concept of the Death Drive and its Relation
to the Superego, Joanne Faulkner
http://www.minerva.mic.ul.ie//vol9/Freud.html